Easter E<

GW00870015

Exploring Easter And Why It Matters

Davo Roberts

Acknowledgements

Editing & Proofing: Roger Kirby

Easter Essentials – version 1.0

Also available on Kindle.

Parts of this book have been previously released with Podcasts and in other PulpTheology books.

Dedication

Firstly, to the Lord our God – Father, Son and Holy Spirit. I wouldn't be here without Him.

Secondly to my wife, Youngmi. She is my one and my only. I can't imagine life without her. I thank God for her daily.

To my father & mother – they could never understand why I needed to believe in God. Yet they taught me to think for myself and to question what people say and teach.

To the unseen millions who have encouraged me just by visiting our Partakers site since 2006, read the items and downloaded the resources. I hope one day that we meet and that I can thank you face to face.

To my Partakers Prayer support team on Facebook – thanks for the prayers, support and for the WOW!

Contents

How To Look Up The Bible 6
Recommended Guidelines.. 7

Introduction 8

1. The Story Leading To Easter 13
2. No Longer A Baby 26
3. Jesus' Final Teaching 36
4. Jesus' Final Prayers 44
5. Jesus' Final Night 52
6. Jesus' Final Breath.. 63
7. Not Down For Long...................................... 72
8. Ready! Set! Go! 83
9. Goings and Comings 89
10. Cross Purposes 95
11. Response Required 111
12. What Is Easter All About? 120

Appendix 1: Who was Jesus? 134
Appendix 2: Assured Atonement.................. 146
Appendix 3: Harmony Of Easter 166

Becoming A Christian 174

Other Books About Jesus By This Author 180
Other Books By This Author 184

How To Look Up The Bible

The following diagram will help you if you are not used to reading the Bible.

Recommended Guidelines

- As you go through each chapter, ask God earnestly to help you understand with your mind, what you are reading. Just speak to him as if you were talking to somebody in the chair next to you. He will help you, if you ask.

- Write down any thoughts or questions that you have in a notebook or on your electronic device, such as a phone or tablet. That way you can come back to them later and/or discuss with somebody else.

- Remember that while you may, or may not, agree with what is written, please do think about why and how what is written is right or wrong.

Introduction

[4] For we died and were buried with Christ by baptism. And just as Christ was raised from the dead by the glorious power of the Father, now we also may live new lives. [5] Since we have been united with him in his death, we will also be raised to life as he was. [6] We know that our old sinful selves were crucified with Christ so that sin might lose its power in our lives. We are no longer slaves to sin. [7] For when we died with Christ, we were set free from the power of sin. [8] And since we died with Christ, we know we will also live with him. [9] We are sure of this because Christ was raised from the dead, and he will never die again. Death no longer has any power over him. [10] When he died, he died once to break the power of sin. But now that he lives, he lives for the glory of God. [11] So you also should consider yourselves to be dead to the power of sin and alive to God through Christ Jesus. (Romans 6:4-11)

Easter. A time when the death and resurrection of the man known as Jesus Christ is remembered and commemorated worldwide. In a lot of people's minds though, Easter doesn't have the same charm and allure as Christmas, when his birth is celebrated. Perhaps that is, in part, due to people being more comfortable when confronted with a baby, than the death of a man. To ease that discomfort we have Easter Eggs being delivered by the Easter Bunny. That is certainly true for those outside of the Church.

No other human birth in history causes more of the world to pause, take a breath and celebrate in different ways. The birth of Jesus Christ caused the world to change. That is what the world celebrates at Christmas. The man this baby would grow into, Jesus Christ, is the most talked about person in history. Almost everyone has an opinion about him.

Yet, who was he, what did he do and what has he to do with us today, some 2,000 years after his birth? When the human we know as Jesus Christ was born, his name imbued the very reason he was born. His conception and birth were extraordinary at every level. Jesus was born to confirm God's promises, invite people into his Sonship, therefore revealing God as a loving Father, and to be our representative before him. He gave us an example of how to live a holy life to the full. Jesus was not merely a man who received some special power, nor was he some strange creation that was half man and half God. He was much more than those ideas as we will see together. The festival of Easter tells the story of Jesus' final days here on earth – his death, resurrection from the dead and his ascension.

The Gospels

What we call the Gospels in the New Testament section of the Bible, give us some details of the life of Jesus Christ as well as telling us some of the theology of the early Church. There are four gospels: Matthew, Mark, Luke and John. They are named after the person thought to have written them. The Gospel of Luke is a partner to the Book of Acts and written by the same person.

Matthew wrote primarily to Jews, presenting Jesus as the long waited for Messiah, predicted in the Old Testament. He also records Israel's attitude towards Jesus as Messiah. Matthew gives us the genealogy of Jesus and proceeds to tell us about Jesus' presentation and authentication as the Messiah. Matthew tells of Israel's opposition to and rejection of Jesus as the Messiah. This causes Jesus to reject Israel due to her unbelief. Matthew then records the death and resurrection of Jesus before concluding with Jesus commissioning the disciples for what we call the Great Commission.

Mark presents Jesus as the Servant of the Lord, coming in fulfilment of Old Testament prophecies. Jesus offers his miracles and his teaching as his credentials and he gathers his disciples, while proclaiming the Kingdom of God. Jesus teaches in short parables, which hide the truth from those hardened against him, while at the same time preparing and instructing those responsive to him. Jesus calls those who follow him to serve him by serving others and to deny themselves by taking up their own Cross, just as he took up his. There is little about the resurrection in this Gospel, possibly because the end of the scroll has been lost.

Luke in his gospel, presents Jesus as the God-Man, a Saviour for the entire world. He writes primarily for Gentiles in the Roman and Greek world. He does this from a broad vantage point that is compatible with the fact that he is himself Greek. Luke traces Jesus' incarnation, introduction, public ministry, rejection, subsequent teaching in view of his rejection, the Cross, resurrection and ascension. Even though a Gentile, Luke emphasizes the kingdom program, with Israel's place in the kingdom. However, he makes it abundantly clear that the kingdom is for all people – not just Israel.

John was writing his Gospel sometime after the other three writers, probably about AD 90. He had built up a considerable fellowship of disciples for whom he was now writing, so John is also concerned with the meaning of what happened behind the events. John presents the person and work of Jesus Christ in such a way that everyone should believe in Jesus as the Son of God, the Messiah, the Saviour of the world. John's argument portrays Jesus as the God-Man, recording as he does the miracles and messages which affirm both Jesus' deity and humanity. John builds his record around Jesus' public ministry, private ministry, the Cross and the resurrection. The result is a Gospel worthy of much careful thought and meditation.

Acts: In this the second of his writings, Luke records Jesus' return to be with the Father and the coming of the promised Holy Spirit to guide the Church and believers. Luke also relates the story of the Church following Jesus' resurrection and ascension. It is the historical record of the beginning, scattering, adjusting, expansion and edification of the Church. Luke's record here presents the development of the one body of Christ consisting of both believing Jews and Gentiles.

1. The Story Leading To Easter

The story of God's dealings with humanity can be see quite easily in a broad way by looking at his dealings with humanity in history, particularly in the covenants that were made between God and humanity.

In the Bible, covenants were common in all kinds of life. Not only between God and humanity. In Old Testament times, it was standard practice for a more powerful nation to have client nations. The senior nation, or suzerain as it was called, would promise to protect the weaker nation if it was attacked; the weaker nation would promise to supply troops to the suzerain on demand, if it or one of the other client nations was attacked. There would be tax liabilities too. It was a very mutual and supportive arrangement. It was ideally placed to serve as the example of how God would support those who promised to honour and serve Him.

There are many covenants in the Bible between God and humanity which showed God promising to do something and commands for humanity to follow. When an Old Testament covenant ended in failure, it was always due to humanity's inability to obey God. Such as when Adam and Eve ate the fruit of the tree of the knowledge of good and evil, thereby breaking the covenant God had made with them. What is known as the Edenic Covenant was therefore terminated and now God needed to make another covenant with Adam (Genesis 3:14-21). In the Old Testament, there are six covenants between God and humanity: Edenic, Adamic, Noahic, Abrahamic, Mosaic, and the Davidic, although some theologies only emphasise the Abrahamic and Mosaic. Each of them contained the following characteristics:

- God always took the initiative.
- God always gave his solemn promise to fulfil his promise.
- God always waited for a free response from humanity, without coercion or force.

Covenant with Adam & Eve (Genesis 2:15-17)

This was the first covenant between God and man. Adam is commanded in the Edenic Covenant to

- Populate the earth (Genesis 1:28)
- Subjugate the earth (Genesis 1:28)
- Exercise dominion over animals (Genesis 1:28)
- Tend and enjoy the garden of Eden (Genesis 1:29; 2:15)
- Refrain from eating the fruit of the tree of the knowledge of good and evil (Genesis 2:16-17).

When Adam & Eve ate the fruit of the tree of the knowledge of good and evil, the Covenant was terminated, and consequently their spiritual and physical deaths. This failure required God to make a new covenant with Adam.

Covenant with Adam (Genesis 3:14-21)

This second covenant between God and humanity, is also titled the covenant with all of mankind, as it lay down the terms and conditions which hold until sin's curse is lifted (Isaiah 11:6-10; Romans 8:18-23). Because of Adam's sin, all of humanity is born under the curse of sin. The terms and conditions of this covenant include:

- Satan is judged and although he enjoys limited & temporal success (Genesis 3:15), but he will be judged (Genesis 3:15).
- The first Messianic prophecy is given (Genesis 3:15)
- Childbirth now involves pain and the woman is made subject to her husband (Genesis 3:16)
- The ground is cursed, and weeds will grow amongst man's food (Genesis 3:v17 - 19)
- Physical changes occur and now people sweat when they work all their life (Genesis 3:19)
- Because of their sin, people die physically and will also die spiritually (Genesis 3:19)
  - .

Covenant with Noah (Genesis 9:1-19)

This is the third covenant between God and man given after the flood had wiped out earth's population, apart from Noah and his family.

The terms of the Noahic covenant are:

- Populate the earth is reaffirmed (Genesis 9:1).
- Subjection of the animals to humans is reaffirmed (Genesis 9:2).
- Humans are allowed to eat animal flesh but are to refrain from drinking/eating the blood (Genesis 9:3-4)
- Human life's sanctity is established. (Genesis 9:v5, 6).
- God promises to never to destroy the earth again by flood (Genesis 9:11). But as 2 Peter 3:10 tells us, God will destroy it by fire!
- The rainbow is given as a symbol of this covenant and its existence (Genesis 9:12-17)

Covenant with Abraham (Genesis 12:1-3)

Whilst the Edenic, Adamic and Noahic Covenants were universal covenants, the fourth Covenant is the first covenant which is theocratic, or relating to the rule of God. It is dependent on God alone, who by means of grace in the "I will," to bestow promised blessings.

This Abrahamic Covenant is also the basis for the theocratic covenants which follow and provides blessings in three levels:

- National level: "I will make you into a great nation." (Genesis 12:2)
- Personal level: "I will bless you and make you famous, and you will be a blessing to others." (Genesis 12:2)
- Universal level: "All the families on earth will be blessed through you." (Genesis 12:3)

Initially this covenant was in broad outline, but God later confirmed it to Abraham in greater detail (Genesis 13:14-7; 15:1-7, 18-21; 17:1-8). The covenant is a link to all of God's activities and programs until the end of time, when Jesus returns to gather his people to himself.

There were personal aspects of this Covenant, particular in relation to Abraham. These aspects were:

- father of a great nation (Genesis 12:1)
- receive personal blessing (Genesis 12:2)
- receive personal honour and reputation (Genesis 12:2)
- He will be a source of blessing to others. (Genesis 12:3)

The aspects of the Abrahamic Covenant, pertinent universally are:

- blessings on those who bless Abraham and the nation of Israel which comes from him (Genesis 12:3)
- curses on those who curse Abraham and Israel (Genesis 12:3)
- blessings on all the earth through the God's coming Messiah, who is Abraham's son and brings universal salvation. (Genesis 12:1-3 and Galatians 3:8)

Covenant with Moses (Exodus 19:5-8)

This is the fifth covenant between God and humanity and also the second theocratic. It commences with the stipulation:

> [5] "Now if you will obey me and keep my covenant, you will be my own special treasure from among all the peoples on earth; for all the earth belongs to me."
> (Exodus 19:5)

This covenant was to the nation of Israel in order that those who believed God's promise to Abraham, could know how to live righteously. This Mosaic covenant covered the three areas of life:

- The commandments were given so they would know how to correctly relate socially to God (Exodus 20:1-6)
- The judgements were given in order that they could relate socially to each other properly (Exodus 21:1 - 24:11)
- The decrees dictate their religious life so that God could be approached by humanity on his terms (Exodus 24:12 - 31:18).

This Mosaic Covenant, however, does not replace the Abrahamic Covenant, but rather as an addition (Galatians 3:19) to it, until the Messiah

Christ came and made the perfect sacrifice (Galatians 3:17-19). The Covenants pointed towards this momentous event. The Mosaic Covenant was never meant as a means towards salvation. It was given that they could realize their helplessness of their own efforts, and their need of God's help. This Law was only a protective fence until through the promised Messiah, humanity could be made right with God through faith alone and that a work of God's twin wellsprings of grace and mercy.

Covenant with David (2 Samuel 7:4-17)

This covenant with David, is the sixth covenant and third theocratic covenant and promises three things :
- A land forever (2 Samuel 7:10)
- A dynasty without end (2 Samuel 7:11, 16)
- A perpetual kingdom (2 Samuel 7:13, 16)

2 Samuel 7:12 predicted the birth of Solomon as David's successor to the throne with his role being to establish David's throne forever (2 Samuel 7:13). We see this link to Jesus Christ, through the genealogies to both Joseph: a legal right to David's throne (Matthew 1:1-17) and to Mary: a blood right to David's throne (Luke 3:23-38).

The Adamic, Noahic and Abrahamic Covenants all looked forward to the coming of the Messiah, as did the Mosaic and Davidic Covenants. All of history points to the coming of this Messiah. This was of course all part of Paul's reasoning from Scripture with the Jews that he came in contact with.

⁶ He has enabled us to be ministers of his new covenant. This is a covenant not of written laws, but of the Spirit. The old written covenant ends in death; but under the new covenant, the Spirit gives life.

⁷ The old way, with laws etched in stone, led to death, though it began with such glory that the people of Israel could not bear to look at Moses' face. For his face shone with the glory of God, even though the brightness was already fading away. ⁸ Shouldn't we expect far greater glory under the new way, now that the Holy Spirit is giving life?

(2 Corinthians 3:6-8)

There would be a new Covenant required, which all the Covenants of the Old Testament pointed towards.

New Covenant

[31] "The day is coming," says the LORD, "when I will make a new covenant with the people of Israel and Judah. [32] This covenant will not be like the one I made with their ancestors when I took them by the hand and brought them out of the land of Egypt. They broke that covenant, though I loved them as a husband loves his wife," says the LORD.
[33] "But this is the new covenant I will make with the people of Israel after those days," says the LORD. "I will put my instructions deep within them, and I will write them on their hearts. I will be their God, and they will be my people.
[34] And they will not need to teach their neighbours, nor will they need to teach their relatives, saying, 'You should know the LORD.' For everyone, from the least to the greatest, will know me already," says the LORD. "And I will forgive their wickedness, and I will never again remember their sins."
(Jeremiah 31:31-34)
The five features of this covenant are:

- God being your God and you being His
- God forgiving you your sins and they are removed by Him
- God transforming you
- God living inside you and leading you
- The Communion service at the Lord's Table is the enduring mark of the Covenant as we remember Jesus, as he commanded.

This New Covenant is sealed only through the perfect sacrifice of Jesus Christ on the Cross, which we celebrate at Easter. His blood ensures the truth of this New Covenant. There was no other way for this New Covenant to be sealed except through Jesus' blood alone.

This New Covenant finalizes what the Covenant with Moses could only point towards, in which the follower of God is in a dynamic and intimate relationship with God and living a life which conforms to God's holy character. So we must ask, "How was Jesus this Messiah?"

2. No Longer A Baby

As the time drew near for him to ascend to heaven, Jesus resolutely set out for Jerusalem. (Luke 9:51)

Jesus has set his face towards Jerusalem because he knew that was where he was going to die and where his mission would be accomplished. It was there that his true identity would finally be revealed. But what was Jesus' mission and what was his true identity, apart from the obvious of being the son of a carpenter from Nazareth.

Mission

[42] Early the next morning Jesus went out to an isolated place. The crowds searched everywhere for him, and when they finally found him, they begged him not to leave them. [43] But he replied, "I must preach the Good News of the Kingdom of God in other towns, too, because that is why I was sent." [44] So he continued to travel around, preaching in synagogues throughout Judea.
(Luke 4:42-44)

This is the beginning of Jesus' public ministry with a mission is to preach God's Kingdom. A very reluctant John the Baptist baptized him, and the crowds heard God the Father speaking to him. He underwent temptations by the arch-seducer, satan, and emerged victorious from that ordeal. satan waited for another time to try again.

Jesus at home (Luke 4:14-30)

Now Jesus, led by the Holy Spirit, has returned home to Galilee and back in home-territory (Luke 4:14). Because of the power of his teaching, Jesus is becoming known as a great teacher (Luke 4:15). Jesus spent some time in Galilee, become known and is arousing the interest, curiosity and excitement of people.

Worshipping (Luke 4:14-18)

It was Jesus' habit to attend public worship wherever he was. He would have worshipped as any Jewish man would have in the local synagogue.

A typical synagogue service involved:
- Opened with a prayer for God's blessing
- Traditional Hebrew confession of faith (Deuteronomy 6:4-9; 11:13-21)
- Prayer and readings from the Law and the Prophets
- Brief talk given by one of the men or a visiting rabbi (Acts 13:14-16)
- Benediction or prayer

Because of his growing renown as a teacher, it is no surprise that Jesus should be asked to read the Scripture and then to give a short teaching session regarding it. That was the custom in the synagogues at the time. Here in Nazareth, Jesus declared that the day for demonstrating God's salvation had arrived and the day which the prophets looked forward to, was going to be fulfilled (Luke 4:20). He was the Servant, who Isaiah had talked about long ago (Isaiah 61:1-2). Jesus' ministry was divinely directed.

Acceptable Year of the Lord

We see that it was a ministry which gave hope to people who would accept it and also liberated those who were spiritually oppressed (Luke 4:18). When Jesus said in Luke 4:19, that it was he was sent "that the time of the LORD's favour has come.", Jesus was referring to the "Year of Jubilee" (Leviticus 25). This was when every fifty years, the economic system of Israel was balanced. This meant that slaves were set free to be returned to their families and when all financial debts were cancelled. Property that was sold, reverted back to the original owners. Lands were lay bare so that they could rest and rejoice in the Lord.

The local reaction to this announcement by Jesus, was at first one of astonishment (Luke 4:22) and telling each other, "He was the son of Joseph!". Or so they thought. But as we know, Jesus was not the genetical son of Joseph, but rather the Son of God, the new Adam and the founder of a new humanity as Luke goes on to explain. Joseph was, in reality, more like Jesus' step-father.

Rejected (Luke 4:20-30)

These people, particularly the religious leadership, saw Jesus as merely the son of Joseph. Admiration turned to anger, because Jesus began to remind them of God's goodness to the Gentiles.

- The prophet Elijah bypassed all the Jewish widows and helped a Gentile widow in Sidon (1 Kings 17:8-16)
- Elisha healed a Gentile leper from Syria (2 Kings 5:1-15)

Whilst those in Nazareth could only see Jesus in the local setting, he told them his mission was for all Israel! And if Israel rejected this message of Good News, then the Gentiles would be blessed by it (Luke 4:25-27). Upon hearing this, the astonished admiration turned to furious anger (Luke 4:28-30)! Salvation is no longer restricted to Israel but for every child of Adam – every human. Jesus' mission was not to be Israel's Saviour but the world's Saviour. When Jesus quoted the proverb "no prophet is accepted in his own hometown.", he revealed his knowledge of Old Testament history. He knew that God's messengers often were rejected, and even as God's Son, he was rejected as well.

Jesus' mission was to be the Saviour of the world as God's Son (John 3:16) and the Servant of the Lord. His mission was to give a message of hope for the spiritually poor and spiritually oppressed people. Not only people in his hometown, nor only in the nation of Israel, but rather for the whole world. People have two choices when faced with this fact: accept or reject. There is no other option. Which choice have you made, if indeed, you have made a choice knowingly?

Identity

And what of his identity? Who was Jesus? In Mark 8:27-33, we read that Jesus asked his disciples, "Who do people say I am?"

This section of the Bible contains the verse, when Peter identifies Jesus as the Christ or Messiah or Saviour (Mark 8:29). This is a call from Peter, which publicly divulges Jesus' true identity, In the preceding few verses Jesus and the disciples were in Bethsaida and there is the incident where Jesus healed the blind man. When the man is healed,

Jesus instructs the man not to tell anybody! Why did Jesus stipulate that? I believe it was because Jesus didn't want to be seen as simply only a healer and miracle worker. He was certainly more than just that.

Confess who Jesus is

In answering the question given to them by Jesus, the disciples gave two answers to Jesus' question. Firstly some say John the Baptist. However, this was untenable due to the following reasons:

- Jesus and John had been seen together in public and they were different in personality and ministry
- John came 'in the spirit and power of Elijah' (Luke 1:17), in a ministry of judgement, whereas Jesus came in a spirit of meekness and service.
- John performed no miracles (John 10:41), but Jesus was a miracle worker.
- John even dressed like the Prophet Elijah (2 Kings 1:8; Mark 1:6)

Ergo, Jesus could not possibly be John the Baptist. The disciples continue by repeating local gossip which stated that Jesus was somehow none other than Jeremiah the prophet, (Matthew 16:14).

- Jeremiah was the 'weeping prophet', and Jesus was the 'man of sorrows'
- Jeremiah called the people to true repentance from the heart, and so did Jesus.
- Both men were misunderstood and rejected by their own people.
- Both men condemned the false religious leaders and the hypocritical worship in the temple.
- Those in authority persecuted both men.

Clearly though, Jesus could not have been Jeremiah, any more than he could have been John the Baptist, despite the circulating rumours and gossip. In both his works and words, Jesus gave evidence to the people that he was indeed the Son of God, the Messiah, and yet they did not get the message. The disciples had much to learn about him and what it meant to follow him. The Jews were expecting a victorious Messiah (Isaiah 11:1-5). But they had forgotten that the Messiah must also suffer and die (Isaiah 53:1-12; Luke 24:26). The Jewish people thought that the Messiah would set up an earthly political kingdom, but Jesus came to set up a spiritual kingdom that would last forever (Isaiah 9:7; Daniel 7:13-14; Luke 1:33; Revelation 11:15)

What was the purpose of the Messiah?

Jesus' mission was to be the Servant of the Lord (Mark 10:45), and therefore, the Saviour of the world as God's Son (John 3:16). His purpose as the Messiah was neither that he be served nor that he will lead a political overthrow of the Roman government as some had hoped. Rather, his purpose as the Messiah, the Saviour, was to be God's servant and give a message of hope for the spiritually poor and spiritually oppressed people.

Follow who Jesus is

When Jesus rebuked Peter, he was also telling off the other disciples (Mark 8:33). Remember that they did not yet understand the relationship between suffering and glory. By the time Peter had written what we know as his first letter, 1 Peter, he did know, as well as who Jesus really was (1 Peter1:6-8, 1 Peter 4:13-5:10).

- Some Jewish leaders taught of 2 Messiahs – one to suffer and one who would reign
- (1 Peter 1:10-12)
- There is a price to pay for true followers:
- Surrender completely to Him.
- Identify with him in his suffering and death.
- Follow him obediently, wherever he leads.

A further question now. What is the reward for the true disciple of Jesus? The prince of this world, satan promises glory now, but in the end suffering comes. However, God promises suffering now, but the suffering turns to glory.

Spiritually, at this time, the disciples were still blind to who Jesus was, just as the man who was physically blind. Our confession of Jesus is a matter of life and death (John 8:21;1 John 4:1-3). The confession of Jesus as Lord is necessary for salvation (1 Corinthians 12:1-3), when that confession is from the heart (Romans 10:9-10). Christians are called to follow Jesus, to take up their Cross and this could mean nothing less than being ready to suffer and die for Jesus. If we are ashamed of him on earth, he will be ashamed of us when the end of the world has come. He will reward those deserving the reward, and deny those who deny Him.

3. Jesus' Final Teaching

5 "But now I am going away to the one who sent me, and not one of you is asking where I am going. 6 Instead, you grieve because of what I've told you. 7 But in fact, it is best for you that I go away, because if I don't, the Advocate won't come. If I do go away, then I will send him to you. 8 And when he comes, he will convict the world of its sin, and of God's righteousness, and of the coming judgment. 9 The world's sin is that it refuses to believe in me. 10 Righteousness is available because I go to the Father, and you will see me no more. 11 Judgment will come because the ruler of this world has already been judged.

(John 16:5-11)

With Jesus' mission and identity clearly in mind, let's now go to look at Jesus' last formal teaching session before he goes to the Cross. In this last little while before he is crucified, Jesus is saying goodbye to his disciples and giving them some final teaching before he departs. Several times he has told them that he is going away to be arrested, betrayed, condemned and crucified (John 13:33; John 14:3-4, 19, 28).

Of course, everything Jesus did in his earthly ministry, involved a lesson to be learnt. There are other events such as Peter's denials and subsequent repentance, where we can also learn lessons. But this chapter is Jesus' final active session of teaching his disciples. So what does he teach them?

Disciples must bear fruit for the kingdom

[1] "I am the true grapevine, and my Father is the gardener. [2] He cuts off every branch of mine that doesn't produce fruit, and he prunes the branches that do bear fruit so they will produce even more."
(John 15:1-2)

As usual Jesus uses Old Testament language, for in the Old Testament, the nation of Israel is often seen as a vine (Jeremiah 2:21; Psalm 80). However as a vine, Israel had not produced the fruit which God had expected, as explained by Isaiah:

[1] Now I will sing for the one I love
a song about his vineyard:
My beloved had a vineyard
on a rich and fertile hill.
[2] He ploughed the land, cleared its stones,
and planted it with the best vines.
In the middle he built a watchtower
and carved a winepress in the nearby rocks.
Then he waited for a harvest of sweet grapes,
but the grapes that grew were bitter.
(Isaiah 5:1-2)

With Jesus describing himself as the true Vine, the implication is clear that the nation of Israel was but an imperfect precursor to his perfect self. With Jesus as the vine, all believers are the branches, and all believers draw spiritual nourishment from him. As part of this nourishment, sometimes pruning is required (John 15:2). Cleansing is also required in order that fruit be borne from the Christian Disciple. This cleansing is through regular confession of sin and partaking of Holy Communion as explained in the foot-washing scene of John 13. To prove to others they are his followers and his disciples, Jesus tells them they are to continue loving him and also to sacrificially love others joyfully (John 15:12-14). By doing these things, which is now their mission statement, they will bear much good fruit for God's greater glory (John 15:8).

Disciples will suffer for the kingdom (John 15:18-27)

Having spoken of love and bearing fruit, Jesus now declares a warning and the context into which he is sending them. We learn from this passage that opposition to Jesus' message is unavoidable. The first opposition is that of the old nature attacking the new nature. Christian Disciples, Jesus said, were called out from the world (John 15:19). Christian Disciples upon conversion belong to a different place and are heading for a different place

Secondly, opposition is to be expected simply because of who Jesus is (John 15:21). Christian Disciples share in the life of Jesus and the way the world treats Jesus is the way the world treats all his disciples (John 15:20-21).

Thirdly, opposition comes through revealing evil. Jesus, as the Light of the World, exposed evil and sin through his words (John 15:22) and works (John 15:24). At the beginning of his ministry, Jesus commanded all those who follow him, to also be "lights of the world" (Matthew 5:14-16). This is done by consistently ensuring that our works and words match our lifestyle and that no hypocrisy will be found. Opposition brings persecution, and regularly throughout history, Christian believers have been persecuted for their faith in Jesus. In our own time, perhaps the most persecuted century of all.

Being a Christian is not an easy decision, but it is worth it. It is also endurable because of three things: God still remains Lord God despite all; .we share in Jesus' own sufferings and therefore have fellowship with him (Philippians 3:10) and by being persecuted, it shows we belong to him (John 15:19).

The main reason all opposition can be endured is because the Christian Disciple is not alone. God the Holy Spirit witnesses with the Christian Disciple (John 15:26). Not as a supplementary person filling a perfunctory role, but rather as the pioneer going out to testify about Jesus ahead (John 15:26) of the Christian Disciple (John 15:27).

Disciples will have resources in the Kingdom (John 16)

The first resource that Christian Disciples have is, the Holy Spirit. After all, he is the real evangelist. In conjunction with him, the Christian Disciple has three resources to use: proclaiming, counselling and discipling.

a. Proclaiming (John 16:1-7): this is the proclaiming and elucidating work about Jesus that the Spirit performs. The Holy Spirit testifies about Jesus' death on the Cross and subsequent resurrection (John 16:14). If Jesus did not go back to glory, and the Holy Spirit was not sent, then the pioneering work of the Holy Spirit would be missing from evangelism and mission. Not only does the Holy Spirit direct people to Jesus, but take them to Him.

b. Counselling (John 16:8-11): As well as proclaiming about Jesus, the Holy Spirit speaks to people's hearts personally – one to one. This signifies the intimacy between the holy God and the believer. The Holy Spirit convinces people hearing God's Word of three things: their own sin (John 16:8); their separation from a holy & righteous God (John 16:10) and also in regard to the judgement of Satan and all who follow him (John 16:11). In these three things, a person is led to the Cross of Christ, in order to confess their sin and their need of Jesus Christ and the salvation only he

c. Discipling (John 16:12-16): Once bought to faith, the Holy Spirit performs several tasks for the Twelve Disciples: he will guide them into all truth and develop what is coming in the future (John

16:13). The New Testament is the product of this work and that through the inspiration of the Holy Spirit. For the Christian Disciple today, the Holy Spirit helps them to apply the Bible to their life in order that Jesus Christ be glorified (John 16:14).

The second resource available to the Christian Disciple is Jesus himself!   Jesus' presence, provision and position.

Presence (John 16:16-33): Yes, his very presence! The twelve disciples will experience sorrow and loss when Jesus is crucified and dead. But after the resurrection, their sorrow will turn to great joy – similar to the exceeding joy after the pains of childbirth! Christian Disciples today also have Jesus' presence with them, particularly when engaged in doing the work of an evangelist!

Provision: Not only his presence, but also his provision! Through answered prayer, joy abounds (John 16:24)! Prayer is going to be of prime importance for the twelve disciples as it is a way to ensure unabated joy – joy even amidst suffering and trouble!

Position: Finally, not only his presence, his provision but also look at his position! Jesus has overcome the world (John 16:33) and nothing can prevail against Him! If you are with Jesus, nothing will prevail against him and he will protect you, provide for you and be with you in all you do, as you submit yourself to him. Whether in the bad times or the good times, Jesus will be with you – but you need to ask him to be with you and rely on him fully. If you are going through bad times now, and don't know this Jesus yet, then ask him to be with you – what have you got to lose?

4. Jesus' Final Prayers

[1] After saying all these things, Jesus looked up to heaven and said, "Father, the hour has come. Glorify your Son so he can give glory back to you. [2] For you have given him authority over everyone. He gives eternal life to each one you have given him. [3] And this is the way to have eternal life—to know you, the only true God, and Jesus Christ, the one you sent to earth. [4] I brought glory to you here on earth by completing the work you gave me to do. [5] Now, Father, bring me into the glory we shared before the world began.

(John 17:1-5)

With Jesus' final teaching in our mind, we now look at Jesus last prayer, talking to God. Firstly praying for himself, then for his twelve disciples and then finally for all disciples of all generations to follow, the Church. This prayer is probably the pinnacle of revelation in John's gospel. Here we see Jesus' very words, revealing an unparalleled intimacy with his Father. This scene, as portrayed by John, shows the importance of prayer and how when doing anything for the glory of God, it must be covered in prayer.

Jesus prays for himself

Central to this part of his prayer is glorification. That is the glorification of himself, in order that God the Father who sent him will be glorified. Glorify is rarely used outside of Church circles today. If ever it is, is usually in the context of somebody pretending to be better than they really are. Glorify means, in a biblical context, to have the person's true nature disclosed. In effect therefore, Jesus is saying in John 17:1: "May people see me for who I truly am, your Son. And may they also through Me, see Your true nature, Father!"

Praying as Jesus does, just before he goes to the Cross, shows the importance of the Cross. For it is through the Cross alone. both God the Father and

Jesus will be glorified. Jesus' death on the Cross reveals a God of love, faithfulness and forgiveness. John 17:4 reveals that it was this purpose that he came, in order to complete the work given. Jesus' entire earthly life has been one to show divine love – to all people of every age and class. All his works and words were completed without even a hint of hypocrisy. His entire life was driven by the desire to see sinful people turn to God for reconciliation and forgiveness.

At the Cross and through the Cross, this is achieved. Jesus confidently prays that having laid aside his glory by taking on human form, he will return to God's right hand, having achieved the work of redemption through the Cross. The theme of eternal life runs throughout John's Gospel (John 3:15-16; John 10:28). Eternal life is knowing God personally and intimately, and that is only achieved by faith through Jesus' death on the Cross. It is a free offer and open to all. It is the responsibility of all people to take up the offer. Once the offered is taken up, the responsibility is then to tell others of this offer.

Jesus prays for his Disciples

[6] Jesus told him, "I am the way, the truth, and the life. No one can come to the Father except

through me. [7] If you had really known me, you would know who my Father is. From now on, you do know him and have seen Him!"

[8] Philip said, "Lord, show us the Father, and we will be satisfied."

(John 14:6-8)

In this part of the prayer, Jesus prays for his disciples. Note how Jesus describes that they were chosen by God himself, had seen God in Jesus, received God's words from Jesus and obeyed them (John 17:6). John 17:6, 9-10 tells us that the disciples were in the safe possession of both the Father and the Son. John 17:7-8 shows what the disciples know. Despite misunderstanding frequently what Jesus was talking about, the disciples still grasped that Jesus had come from God.

Having taught that they will endure persecution and suffering because they are his followers, Jesus prays for their safety. They will be safe, not because of their own cunning, character or conduct. They will be safe because of God's care and protection (John 17:11-12).

As they are God's possession, he will ensure that they are watched over and protected. This security is also borne from glorifying God and being witnesses for him (John 17:10). God is glorified whenever his salvation plan is explained and told.

Who are the disciples' enemies and why do they need protecting (John 17:11-12, 15)? The first enemy is the world who does not know God and is therefore in rebellion against God. The disciples were told of this prior to this prayer. Satan is also an enemy of the disciple and will do all he can to stop God being glorified in the life of the disciple. How will God keep them safe? Their safety comes only through his mighty name and nature.

Jesus also prays that they may be filled with joy (John 17:13) and be dedicated wholly and solely to him. The disciples now have a mission and purpose to fulfil – to tell others of Jesus. This mission though whilst their responsibility is not theirs alone, but is the continuation of Jesus' mission to bring people to reconciliation and relationship with God. Part of that mission is to live a holy life in the power of the Holy Spirit. Living a holy life means living a life not for themselves but for the glory and obedience of Jesus Christ.

Jesus prays for all Christian Disciples

[24] Father, I want these whom you have given me to be with me where I am. Then they can see all the glory you gave me because you loved me even before the world began!

[25] "O righteous Father, the world doesn't know you,

but I do; and these disciples know you sent me. [26] I have revealed you to them, and I will continue to do so. Then your love for me will be in them, and I will be in them."
(John 17:24-26)

Now Jesus prays for all those who, through the work of the disciples, will become his followers. As such, it brings all Christian disciples into intimacy with Jesus and a part of a dynamic relationship with Him. What does Jesus pray for his Church of followers? Jesus prays for unity. That is unity on various levels. Firstly it is unity on the invisible, supernatural level (John 17:21-22). The lives of all Christian disciples are inextricably linked to each other, through the love and obedience of God the Son and God the Father. Christian disciples are united together because Jesus imparts upon them, the glory given to him by God the Father (John 17:22).

This unity is also physical, in so much as through a visible unity, people will come to know Jesus personally and take up the offer of reconciliation with God (John 17:21, 23). This unity is also physically seen, through the telling of the message of reconciliation (John 17:20). That is why different Churches must be seen to work together – a visible sign of unity reflecting the invisible unity.

[12] This is my commandment: Love each other in

the same way I have loved you. [13] There is no greater love than to lay down one's life for one's friends. [14] You are my friends if you do what I command. [15] I no longer call you slaves, because a master doesn't confide in his slaves. Now you are my friends, since I have told you everything the Father told me."
(John 15:12-15)

Much later in his life, John must surely have reflected upon this when he writes:

[16] We know what real love is because Jesus gave up his life for us. So we also ought to give up our lives for our brothers and sisters. [17] If someone has enough money to live well and sees a brother or sister\ in need but shows no compassion—how can God's love be in that person?

[18] Dear children, let's not merely say that we love each other; let us show the truth by our actions. [19] Our actions will show that we belong to the truth, so we will be confident when we stand before God. [20] Even if we feel guilty, God is greater than our feelings, and he knows everything.

[21] Dear friends, if we don't feel guilty, we can come to God with bold confidence. [22] And we will receive from him whatever we ask because

we obey him and do the things that please Him. [23] And this is his commandment: We must believe in the name of his Son, Jesus Christ, and love one another, just as he commanded us. [24] Those who obey God's commandments remain in fellowship with him, and he with them. And we know he lives in us because the Spirit he gave us lives in us.
(1 John 3:16-24)

If the world sees Christian Disciples loving others sacrificially, then unity is seen and it is an effective witness to the reality of reconciliation with God, and a vibrant living relationship with him. It is also imperative that prayer covers all the work of the Church and the Christian – prayer is the foundation and the backbone, just as prayer strengthened Jesus as he faced the Cross. Without praying so earnestly that he sweated drops of blood, do you think he could have maintained the Cross and its supreme significance for humanity?

5. Jesus' Final Night

[14] Then Jesus returned to Galilee, filled with the Holy Spirit's power. Reports about him spread quickly through the whole region. [15] he taught regularly in their synagogues and was praised by everyone. [16] When he came to the village of Nazareth, his boyhood home, he went as usual to the synagogue on the Sabbath and stood up to read the Scriptures. [17] The scroll of Isaiah the prophet was handed to him. He unrolled the scroll and found the place where this was written: [18] "The Spirit of the LORD is upon me, for he has anointed me to bring Good News to the poor. He has sent me to proclaim that captives will be released, that the blind will see, that the oppressed will be set free, [19] and that the time of the LORD's favour has come." [20] He rolled up the scroll, handed it back to the attendant, and sat down. All eyes in the synagogue looked at him intently. [21] Then he began to speak to them. "The Scripture you've just heard has been fulfilled this very day!" [22] Everyone spoke well of him and was amazed by the gracious words that came from his lips. "How can this be?" they asked. "Isn't this Joseph's son?"
(Luke 4:16-22)

Jesus' public ministry commenced with a bang, in the town where he was raised and known. From that time till his last night, during his 3 years of ministry, Jesus has preached the good news of God's salvation to reconcile people back into relationship with Almighty God. Through the Cross, his mission will be fulfilled.

Passover, Pentecost and Feast of Tabernacles were the three most important feasts on the Jewish calendar (Leviticus 21). All Jewish men were expected to visit Jerusalem (Deuteronomy 16:16). The Passover Feast was to commemorate the deliverance of Israel from Egypt, and it was a time for remembering and rejoicing (Exodus 11-12). Of all the events that took place that night, we will look at just three of them.

Jesus Plans

[1] The Festival of Unleavened Bread, which is also called Passover, was approaching. [2] The leading priests and teachers of religious law were plotting how to kill Jesus, but they were afraid of the people's reaction.

[3] Then Satan entered into Judas Iscariot, who was one of the twelve disciples, [4] and he went to the leading priests and captains of the Temple guard to discuss the best way to betray Jesus to

them. [5] They were delighted, and they promised to give him money. [6] So he agreed and began looking for an opportunity to betray Jesus so they could arrest him when the crowds weren't around.

(Luke 22:1-4)

Jewish people were expected to remove all yeast from their houses (Exodus 12:15) as a reminder that their ancestors left Egypt in a hurry and had to eat bread without yeast. Jesus had warned his disciples about the duplicitous Pharisees when he said, "Beware of the yeast of the Pharisees—their hypocrisy." (Luke 12:1). In other words, the religious leaders had cleansed their houses but not their hearts.

The last thing the religious leaders wanted was a messianic uprising during Passover (Luke 19:11). Judas was motivated and energized by satan (John 13:2, 27) and was never a true believer because his sins had never been cleansed by the Lord (John 13:10-11), therefore Judas had never believed or received eternal life (John 6:64-71). However, it should be noted that Judas had been given authority and had been preaching the same message as the other disciples. This shows just how close a person can come to the kingdom of God and still be lost and not included (Matthew 7:21-29)

Jesus Prepares

[26] As they were eating, Jesus took some bread and blessed it. Then he broke it in pieces and gave it to the disciples, saying, "Take this and eat it, for this is my body."

[27] And he took a cup of wine and gave thanks to God for it. He gave it to them and said, "Each of you drink from it, [28] for this is my blood, which confirms the covenant between God and his people. It is poured out as a sacrifice to forgive the sins of many. [29] Mark my words—I will not drink wine again until the day I drink it new with you in my Father's Kingdom."

[30] Then they sang a hymn and went out to the Mount of Olives.

(Matthew 26:26-30)

The disciples needed a room within Jerusalem itself, and also required food - a lamb, bread, bitter herbs and wine. The Passover meal contains historical and theological symbolism regarding the death of Jesus. This is why this meal is the model for the central act of Christian worship, which is Holy Communion. Here is an outline of a Passover meal at the time of Jesus:

- Opening Prayer
- First cup of wine

- A dish of herbs and sauce
- Story of the Passover recited
- Psalm 113 was sung
- Second cup of wine
- Prayer of Grace
- Main course of roast lamb with unleavened bread and bitter herbs
- A further prayer
- Third cup of wine.
- Psalm 114 to 118 were then sung
- Fourth cup of wine

Depending on your Church, it can be called amongst other things, the Eucharist or The Lord's Supper. Christian Disciples are commanded to participate, as Jesus said: "This is my body, which is given for you. Do this in remembrance of me." (Luke 22:19).

Some Churches do it every service and others do it monthly. Whenever we participate in it, we do it regularly as a remembrance of Jesus until he comes again (1 Corinthians 11:26). The bread symbolizes his body broken on the Cross and the wine symbolizes his blood which was shed on the Cross. Therefore before we partake of the bread and wine, we are to examine ourselves and confess any unforgiven sin (1 Corinthians 11:28-29). This is done because it would be hypocritical to eat it while harbouring known sin in our hearts and having fellowship with Jesus and others in the Church!

This Last Supper, the Holy Communion – what is its significance for us?

- It symbolizes fellowship with other believers in the universal Church (1 Corinthians 10:17)
- We receive the benefits of his once and for all sacrifice (1 Corinthians 10:16)
- We spiritually feed upon Christ (1 Corinthians 11:24)
- It symbolizes the death of Christ for our sin (Luke 22:19)
- It symbolizes our acceptance of Christ's death for us
- It symbolizes our dependence on Christ for spiritual life

When a person remembers, that makes it their own personal story. If something is only recalled as an historical event, then that is somebody else's story being recalled. That is why Holy Communion is personal – it's our story! Is it yours also?

All these symbolize the New Covenant made between God and Jesus' Disciples – a Covenant guaranteeing salvation! The new covenant is a new meal, in order to remind his followers in every age about the work of Jesus Christ on the Cross. The

New Covenant (Luke 22:20), Jesus claims that his death, was spoken about by the prophets Jeremiah (Jeremiah 31:33-34) and Ezekiel.

It was a new covenant in which God's people will be able to know him intimately for their sins will be forgiven. Whenever a covenant was made between God and man, blood was always shed. Jesus' blood will be the seal on this New Covenant, which is why we remember it. Jesus has moved on from the old and come to do something new!

Two other main views insist that it is more than just symbolic! Firstly, there is transubstantiation, which believes that the bread and wine actually become the blood and body of Jesus Christ.

Secondly there is, consubstantiation, which believes that the body and blood of Christ are present in the Communion meal.

However both of these views would indicate that Jesus Christ is being re-sacrificed, and Hebrews 7 refutes these views, when talking about Jesus' death on the cross:

"Unlike those other high priests, he does not need to offer sacrifices every day. They did this for their own sins first and then for the sins of the people. But Jesus did this once for all when he offered himself as the sacrifice for the people's sins."
(Hebrews 7:27).

The bread we eat and wine we drink at Holy Communion are therefore only symbolic of his sacrifice, not turning into the actual flesh and blood of Jesus Christ and can most assuredly never be a re-enactment.

Jesus Serves

As part of the custom of the day, a servant or slave usually undertook foot washing of guests. Since none of the disciples had done this, Jesus himself undertakes the task (John 13:4-5). Peter is recalcitrant and resistant as always, objects (John 13:6, 8). Peter learns that only those cleansed by Jesus and trusting in him fully, can be a part of the kingdom (John 13:7, 9). As we look back at this episode, knowing what we do now of the Cross, we learn how this simple act of washing feet is symbolic of Jesus' sacrificial death on the Cross.

The Cross and washing of feet are both displays of great love and service. Just as Peter opposed Jesus going to the Cross (Matthew 16:21-23), so he objected to having his feet washed here. Jesus' getting up to serve symbolizes his coming to serve. As he took off his cloak, this symbolizes the taking off of his glory when he became man. Girding himself with a towel, symbolizes his taking on human flesh in the incarnation at his birth. As the water cleansed the feet, so Jesus death and blood cleanse from sin. As he returned to where he was sitting and sat down after finishing this act of service, Jesus returned to the right hand of God after his work on the Cross.

When people become Christian, their sins are forgiven through Jesus' death on the Cross. That is when they had our "bath" as it were. That is the very point when we, if we are Christians, were justified before God and we are declared his child. Having been justified already, we don't need a bath anymore! But we do need the equivalent of a feet washing daily and or every time we take Holy Communion and a cleansing of our sin when we confess it before our God and repent.

Comparing Plans

As we compare and contrast the plan of Jesus and the plans of his enemies, we see a vast gulf between them:

Plans of his enemies

- Plot to kill Jesus (Luke 22:2)
- Arranges Judas to betray Jesus (Luke 22:3)
- Satan's purpose is to destroy Jesus (Luke 22:3, Luke 22:31)

Plans of Jesus

- Jesus is in control
- Plans the Passover meal (Luke 22:7-12)
- The meal is part of his plan (Luke 22:16)
- He knows Judas' plan (Luke 22:21-22)
- Replaces the old leaders of God with his men (Luke 22: 30)

All the elements in the plot conspiring against Jesus had been allowed for. The death of Jesus was no accident.

[18] For you know that God paid a ransom to save you from the empty life you inherited from your ancestors. And it was not paid with mere gold or silver, which lose their value. [19] It was the precious blood of Christ, the sinless, spotless Lamb of God. [20] God chose him as your ransom long before the world began, but now in these last days he has been revealed for your sake.

[21] Through Christ you have come to trust in God. And you have placed your faith and hope in God because he raised Christ from the dead and gave him great glory.

(1 Peter 1:18-21)

After Jesus' last prayers in Gethsemane, one of the disciples, his close companions, Judas, fulfils his betrayal of Jesus to the Romans, with a kiss of greetings, in order to identify Jesus and Jesus is arrested. Jesus is subsequently taken away to be rejected by those closest to him, to face trial, be whipped and crucified.

6. Jesus' Final Breath

[28] Jesus knew that his mission was now finished, and to fulfil Scripture he said, "I am thirsty." [29] A jar of sour wine was sitting there, so they soaked a sponge in it, put it on a hyssop branch, and held it up to his lips. [30] When Jesus had tasted it, he said, "It is finished!" Then he bowed his head and gave up his spirit.

(John 19:28-30)

¹³ See, my servant will prosper;

he will be highly exalted.

¹⁴ But many were amazed when they saw Him.

His face was so disfigured he seemed hardly human,

and from his appearance, one would scarcely know he was a man.

¹⁵ And he will startle many nations.

Kings will stand speechless in his presence.

For they will see what they had not been told;

they will understand what they had not heard about.

(Isaiah 52:13-15)

¹⁰ But it was the LORD's good plan to crush him and cause him grief.

Yet when his life is made an offering for sin,

he will have many descendants.

He will enjoy a long life, and the LORD's good plan will prosper in his hands.

¹¹ When he sees all that is accomplished by his anguish, he will be satisfied.

And because of his experience,

my righteous servant will make it possible

for many to be counted righteous,

for he will bear all their sins.

¹² I will give him the honours of a victorious soldier,

because he exposed himself to death.
He was counted among the rebels.
He bore the sins of many and interceded for rebels.
(Isaiah 53:10-12:)

Those words were spoken of the coming Messiah, by the prophet Isaiah, centuries before Jesus Christ. Together we have looked at during this Easter series, Jesus' mission and identity and have placed him as the Messiah spoken about throughout the Old Testament, including Isaiah. Following his betrayal, Jesus is now facing trial in a Roman court, being interrogated by Pontius Pilate, the Roman Governor.

Jesus was Condemned

Pilate gave in and permitted the flogging and mockery in the hope of shaming Jesus' accusers (John 19:1-3). Pilate affirmed Jesus' innocence after the scourging (John 19:4). Jesus' refusal to answer stung Pilate into reminding Jesus of his Roman authority (John 19:10). Jesus, however, corrected Pilate's idea of authority and told him that although Pilate may have power on earth, his power did reach beyond earth (John 19:11). Jesus knew that his work of bring people back to God in a loving relationship did not rest on the actions of a mere Roman governor. Pilate was more concerned with his own position than he was for justice. In all this, Jesus is seen as the true Passover lamb.

Jesus was Crucified

Jesus bearing his own Cross, was killed as a common criminal (John 19:17). Pilate was responsible for fixing the sign "The King of the Jews" (John 19:21-22) despite protests from the Jewish authorities. The clothes of condemned prisoners were given to soldiers on duty (John 19:23). Even when he himself was in agony, Jesus showed concern for his mother, committing her to the Apostle John (John 19:s.26-27). The crucifixion site was purposely chosen to be outside the city walls because the Law forbade such within the city walls for sanitary reasons. The crucified body was sometimes left to rot on the Cross and serve as a disgrace, a convincing warning and deterrent to passers-by. Sometimes, the subject was eaten while alive and still on the Cross by wild beasts. Jesus face was beaten beyond recognition and the scourging lacerated his flesh. The whips used had pieces of glass and rocks stuck to the cord so as to inflict as much damage as possible. He had a crown of thorns pushed into his scalp.

In Jesus' final moments, he utters "I am thirsty." (John 19:28) and "It is finished." (John 19:30). The desire of the Jewish authorities (John 19:32) to fulfil their rituals was important as the Sabbath fell within the Passover. The breaking of legs (John 19:32-33) sped Jesus' death. The flow of blood and water from the piercing of his side, proved that Jesus was truly dead (John 19:34).

Jesus was Buried

Joseph of Arimithea and Nicodemus buried Jesus. The significance of "never used before." (John 19:41) is to demonstrate that the body of Jesus at no point came into contact with the decay of a dead body. Guards were placed at the tomb to ensure that nobody could tamper with the body or steal it way.

[38] Afterward Joseph of Arimathea, who had been a secret disciple of Jesus
(because he feared the Jewish leaders), asked Pilate for permission to take down Jesus' body. When Pilate gave permission, Joseph came and took the body away. [39] With him came Nicodemus, the man who had come to Jesus at night. He brought about seventy-five pounds of perfumed ointment made from myrrh and

aloes. [40] Following Jewish burial custom, they wrapped Jesus' body with the spices in long sheets of linen cloth. [41] The place of crucifixion was near a garden, where there was a new tomb, never used before. [42] And so, because it was the day of preparation for the Jewish Passover and since the tomb was close at hand, they laid Jesus there.

(John 19:38-42)

It is Saturday. Jesus Christ has been condemned, crucified, died and is buried in an unused tomb. What now? It is the day after. It is the Saturday, which means it is the Sabbath. The Bible is silent about this day. This is the day between the crucifixion and resurrection of Jesus Christ. There isn't a story about the tears shed, the memories shared, the hugs and the hurting hearts. Where are his close followers, the disciples? What of the Jewish authorities? Were they gleeful at the demise of this man Jesus who claimed to be the Messiah? We don't know.

This is a dark day, a day when Jesus did some of the most precious work ever. This is the day when after his physical death he walked through the Valley of the Shadow of Death and he carried all of us. Every sin, every tear, every wound, Jesus carried them all and didn't drop a single one.

Harried and harassed, he fought death and washed us clean. From that last breath to the angelic tomb break he fought for us, he carried us.

We used to have to walk through that valley, until Jesus on that dark Sabbath walked it one last time for us. How wonderful! How amazing. How awesome!

Knowing what we know now, we can see this dark Sabbath for what it really is. But how was it for the sisters, Mary and Martha or for Mary, the mother of Jesus and the other Mary of Magdalene and the other women who were waiting to tend to Him.

Their time was short on that terror filled Friday and they could offer no proper anointing, no proper farewell. A quick bit of tearful heartbroken work before the sun went down. Then a day to wait. The longest, darkest day knowing that he was gone.

Even in the middle of our deepest grief we can find peace. I think these people of Jesus were seeking that peace, together. I wonder how much love they had for each other or how badly they were frightened? I believe that the Holy Spirit quietened their hearts.

I wonder on that dark Sabbath if the members of the Sanhedrin or Pilate and Claudia or Herod were frightened by what they had wrought? Or were they rejoicing that another problem was solved? When did someone find Judas? Did he lay at the bottom of the hill all day, alone and scavenged upon? Possibly. Did anyone mourn that lost soul, besides Jesus? I wonder about the thief who accepted Jesus at the last moment of his life. "Today you will be with me in paradise!" That was the promise. What a promise!

Because of our sins, we all shared the same death sentence as those criminals who flanked our Lord. And yet it was because of those very sins, that he chose to pay our price for freedom. Jesus did what no one else could do - he saved the world from itself. And, wonder of all wonders, he did it willingly and with love. The ultimate love. The perfect love.

That dark Sabbath was washed in tears, blood and yet it claimed no victory. The temple curtain was torn. The old was passed away. That dark Sabbath was the last of its kind. No more innocent lambs to bleed out, potion out and burn. The perfect Lamb took all of our places, forever!

It is fitting that the day of the dark Sabbath had no words spoken about it. It is fitting because everyone needs to catch their breath from the Cross to the empty tomb. It is a huge journey to take, but Jesus no only led the way, but he cleared it, filled it with light and love. Today, as you catch your breath between Good Friday and Easter Sunday think of the quiet darkness of that Sabbath day. Take some time now, to consider what the silence, the tears and the sense of waiting for something amazing must have been like. The world waited, the very creation beneath our feet, just as was beneath theirs, held its breath. Silently.

7. Not Down For Long

[1] Early on Sunday morning, while it was still dark, Mary Magdalene came to the tomb and found that the stone had been rolled away from the entrance. [2] She ran and found Simon Peter and the other disciple, the one whom Jesus loved. She said, "They have taken the Lord's body out of the tomb, and we don't know where they have put him!"

[3] Peter and the other disciple started out for the tomb. [4] They were both running, but the other disciple outran Peter and reached the tomb first. [5] He stooped and looked in and saw the linen wrappings lying there, but he didn't go in. [6] Then Simon Peter arrived and went inside. He also noticed the linen wrappings lying there, [7] while the cloth that had covered Jesus' head was folded up and lying apart from the other wrappings. [8] Then the disciple who had reached the tomb first also went in, and he saw and believed — [9] for until then they still hadn't understood the Scriptures that said Jesus must rise from the dead. [10] Then they went home. (John 20:1-10)

Jesus has risen from the dead! Silent Saturday and the dark Sabbath are over! All four gospel accounts give this great and amazing news! Jesus is no longer dead. He is alive! Can you get a bigger WOW that that? The disciples evidently still didn't fully understand it, but they would very soon. Soon the news would spread and the evidence of this comes from the Apostle Paul.

[1] Let me now remind you, dear brothers and sisters, of the Good News I preached to you before. You welcomed it then, and you still stand firm in it. [2] It is this Good News that saves you if you continue to believe the message that I told you—unless, of course, you believed something that was never true in the first place. [3] I passed on to you what was most important and what had also been passed on to me. Christ died for our sins, just as the Scriptures said. [4] He was buried, and he was raised from the dead on the third day, just as the Scriptures said. [5] He was seen by Peter and then by the Twelve.

[6] After that, he was seen by more than 500 of his followers at one time, most of whom are still alive, though some have died. [7] Then he was seen by James and later by all the apostles. [8] Last of all, as though I had been born at the wrong time, I also saw Him.

(1 Corinthians 15:1-5)

These words were written by the Apostle Paul, to the Corinthian Church, not long after the events of Easter. Here Paul talks about Jesus having been raised from the dead – physically!

All four Gospels, Matthew, Mark Luke and John, tell us that Jesus was crucified, died and was buried in a tomb. What do these four Gospels say about Jesus' physical resurrection or rising from the dead? Let's look at a harmony of those accounts of the events of Jesus' burial, resurrection and post-resurrection appearances. As you look, take note of all the different people involved and the places named.

The tomb is empty

- Two Marys watch the burial: (Matthew27:61, Mark 15:47, Luke23:54-55)
- Roman soldiers guard the tomb and place an official Roman seal upon it: (Matthew 27:62-66)
- Women prepare burial spices then rest: (Luke 23:56)
- An angel rolls the stone away: (Matthew 28:2-4)
- Women arrive at dawn with spices: (Matthew 28:1, Mark 16:1-4, Luke 24:1-3, John 20:1)
- Angels appear to women: (Matthew 28:5-7, Mark 16:5-7, Luke 24:4-8)
- Women dart back to tell disciples: (Matthew 28:8, Mark 16:8, Luke 24:9-11, John 20:2)
- Peter and John investigate the empty tomb: (Luke 24:12, John 20:3-9)
- Peter and John go home: (Luke 24:12, John 20:10)
- Mary Magdalene weeps by the tomb: (John 20:11)
- Mary sees two angels: (John 20:12-13)

Jesus' appearances

- Jesus appears to Mary Magdalene: (Mark 16:9, John 20:14-17)
- Jesus appears to the other women: (Matthew 28:9-10)
- Women report to the disciples: (Mark 16:10-11, John 20:18)
- Guards testify to the priests: (Matthew 28:11-15)
- Jesus meets two people on the Emmaus Road: (Mark 16:12-13, Luke 24:13-32)
- Jesus appears to Simon Peter: (1 Corinthians 15:5, Luke 24:34)
- 2 report to disciples in Jerusalem: (Luke 24:33-35)
- Jesus appears to the Disciples less Thomas: (Luke 24:36-43, John 20:19-24)
- Disciples report to Thomas: (John 20:25)
- Jesus appears to the Disciples and Thomas: (Mark 16:14, John 20:26-29)
- Jesus appears to seven people: (John 21:1-14)
- Jesus questions Peter 3 times: (John 21:15-23)
- Jesus appears to 500 people: (1 Corinthians 15:6)
- Jesus appears to James: (1 Corinthians 15:7)

Evidences for the resurrection

These facts remain for the resurrection. Look at them and study them. Notice the changed attitude of the disciples after seeing the risen Jesus. They changed from defeated, cowardly people to victorious, brave people. Nobody who could have produced the dead body of Jesus, did so. Their silence is as significant as the preaching of the Apostles. Or observe the multiple appearances of Jesus to various numbers of individuals and groups of people at various times of the day and in differing circumstances.

This shows that Jesus' resurrection was physical in nature! Some people say Jesus' resurrection was spiritual in nature but not physical. But the amount of people that saw him physically afterwards dispels that particular myth.

What about the current tangible evidence - the survival and inordinate growth and impact of the early Church and that the Church is still growing 2000 years later. If there was no bodily resurrection of Jesus' would people really have risked persecution and death for knowing a lie? One or two people maybe, but not hundreds and thousands! Certainly, I am sure you would agree, it is intangible. However, what about if Jesus had not risen from the dead. What then?

Dealing with Doubters

Surely the authorities, both Jewish and Roman, would have produced his dead body in order to quench this new movement! But they didn't, and the reason they didn't is because there was no body to produce! Would the disciples have risked death for telling and maintaining a lie about the risen Jesus? They were beaten, confused, defeated and dispersed men until they saw that Jesus truly did rise from the dead. They became a transformed and victorious people. Perhaps somebody (even the disciples) stole the body. Hardly likely, and if that had occurred, for what reason? How would they have got past the Roman Guard and moved the stone a great distance from the tomb? This is the story that the Jewish authorities tried to perpetuate:

[11] As the women were on their way, some of the guards went into the city and told the leading priests what had happened. [12] A meeting with the elders was called, and they decided to give the soldiers a large bribe. [13] They told the soldiers, "You must say, 'Jesus' disciples came during the night while we were sleeping, and they stole his body.' [14] If the governor hears about it, we'll stand up for you, so you won't get in trouble." [15] So the guards accepted the bribe and said what they were told to say. Their story

spread widely among the Jews, and they still tell it today.
(Matthew 28:11-15)

Then we have the swoon theory. Jesus didn't die but merely fainted and recovered consciousness in the tomb. Complete nonsense to suggest that Jesus, battered, requiring medical attention and care, could have inspired his disciples and convinced them that he was the Conqueror of sin and death that he had told them that he was. Besides, how could he have moved the stone in such a poor physical condition. Preposterous, isn't it?

Ah here is another good one! Perhaps, they all went to the wrong tomb. That's it – they went to the wrong tomb. Every single one of them – including the Roman guards! That must be it! Nope! Whilst one person may have gone to a wrong tomb, not everyone would have done. Besides, the gospel accounts tell us that people were waiting outside the tomb where Jesus was buried! Surely Joseph would know which tomb Jesus was buried in, seeing as Joseph actually owned it!

Lastly, it is perpetrated by some that Jesus didn't die on the Cross, but somebody was substituted for him. This is certainly untenable, given the rigidity and strict record keeping of Roman rule and with the eyes of the Jewish hierarchy watching. This conjecture is a lie of satan, because he knows the significance of Jesus having risen physically from the dead. That is what satan is and does. A liar who lies, perpetuates half-truths and deceives.

Significance of the Resurrection

The resurrection of Jesus Christ provided the central theme for the sermons and teaching in the early Church (Acts 1:22; Acts 4:33, Acts 17:18) and certainly within 'Paul-ine' theology. But what significance is there in Jesus' resurrection?

The resurrection proved and vindicated all Jesus' teaching and claims as the suffering Servant and attested to his being fully God and the last Judge of all mankind (Isaiah 53:10-12; Acts 2:36; Acts 3:13-15; Romans 1:4). The resurrection, declared God's approval of Jesus obedient service and the fulfilment of all the Old Testament promises, resulting in forgiveness of sins and salvation being only found in and through Jesus Christ, which was the prime motive for evangelism in the early Church (Acts 2:32, Romans 4:24-25). Jesus' resurrection is a sign of the bodily resurrection for all believers in him, giving a new attitude to death and transforming hopes (1 Corinthians 15:12-58, Romans 8:10, 2 Corinthians

4:14; 1 Peter 1:3 & 21). As the resurrected King, Jesus now intercedes for us and has perfected the redemption of all those who choose to follow him (Romans 5:10; Hebrews 6:20, 1 Peter 1:21).

Finally the resurrection of Jesus' physical body is a sure victory over satan, sin and death. All three are conquered and squashed. Satan is a defeated creature and will do anything to drag people into defeat with him. The power of sin is conquered, and sin's grip is overcome if you are a believer in Jesus Christ. Finally, as I said earlier, death has been beaten, because those who believe and trust in Jesus Christ will live forever with him – death is not the end but a beginning. If Jesus Christ did not physically rise from the dead then as Paul states that if Jesus Christ did not physically rise from the dead, all Christians are the product of the greatest delusional lie and are the most foolish of all people.

[12] But tell me this—since we preach that Christ rose from the dead, why are some of you saying there will be no resurrection of the dead? [13] For if there is no resurrection of the dead, then Christ has not been raised either. [14] And if Christ has not been raised, then all our preaching is useless, and your faith is useless. [15] And we apostles would all be lying about God—for we have said that God raised Christ from the grave. But that can't be true if there is no resurrection

of the dead. [16] And if there is no resurrection of the dead, then Christ has not been raised. [17] And if Christ has not been raised, then your faith is useless, and you are still guilty of your sins. [18] In that case, all who have died believing in Christ are lost! [19] And if our hope in Christ is only for this life, we are more to be pitied than anyone in the world.

[20] But in fact, Christ has been raised from the dead. He is the first of a great harvest of all who have died.

(1 Corinthians 15:12-20)

But that is not the end, as we now go on to see

8. Ready! Set! Go!

[16] Then the eleven disciples left for Galilee, going to the mountain where Jesus had told them to go. [17] When they saw him, they worshiped him—but some of them doubted!

[18] Jesus came and told his disciples, "I have been given all authority in heaven and on earth. [19] Therefore, go and make disciples of all the nations, baptizing them in the name of the Father and the Son and the Holy Spirit. [20] Teach these new disciples to obey all the commands I have given you. And be sure of this: I am with you always, even to the end of the age."

(Matthew 28:16-20)

In some of Jesus' final words before ascending back to the right-hand side of God the Father, Jesus gave specific instructions to his Disciples. They will go on to do as Jesus commanded – go and tell the world about this Jesus and teach them to be his disciples! One of the major themes of Matthew's Gospel is the authority of Jesus. Matthew highlights Jesus' authority in action and not just merely in words. For example, Matthew records Jesus' authority to forgive sins (Matthew 9:6) and Jesus imparted authority to his disciples for a short time when they went on a mission in Matthew 10. Jesus has all the authority in heaven and on earth (Matthew 28:18)! Jesus has authority over all things and all people. Jesus has authority over all spiritual beings, whether angels or demons, as well as over all nations, governments, rulers, and over all earthly and spiritual authorities.

One of the consequences of Easter is that Jesus' authority is passed to his disciples. The disciples could be obedient to God without fear of retribution from those who would seek to harm them, regardless of the circumstances they would find themselves in. That is why they were so bold and why the Church spread quickly and grew outside the tiny nation of Israel to throughout the then known world. If Jesus had not risen from the dead, then the disciples would not have had a story to tell. But Jesus had indeed risen from the dead, and the early Church exploded numerically as the twelve disciples exercised Jesus' authority and his power.

Throughout the Gospel of Matthew, Jesus' authority is a major theme. Where Matthew records Jesus doing miracles, this is to highlight Jesus authority in action and not just merely in words. Matthew records Jesus' authority to forgive sins (Matthew 9:6) and he imparted authority to his disciples for a short time when they went on a mission in Matthew 10.

His disciples.

[19] Therefore go and make disciples of all nations, baptising them in the name of the Father and of the Son and of the Holy Spirit, [20] and teaching them to obey everything I have commanded you. And surely, I am with you always, to the very end of the age.'
(Matthew 28:18-20)

Jesus has authority (Matthew 28:18) over all things, all people, all circumstances and happenings including authority over all spiritual beings, whether angels or demons. Jesus has authority over all nations, governments and rulers. Jesus has authority over all earthly and spiritual authorities. Jesus has the authority. This means regardless of whatever the Christian Disciple faces; Jesus is in control. I know that it is very easy to forget this fact!

Therefore, as Christian Disciples today, we can obey him without fear of retribution from those who would seek to harm us. We can obey him regardless of the circumstances we find ourselves in. It is a great comfort to know, that he is in control of everything. Through his death on the Cross and his rising from the dead, Jesus has conquered all enemies. People often confuse authority with authoritarian. Authoritarian means severe, rigidity and a dictator.

None of these applies to Jesus. We have been given a free will, but as his Disciples, we should choose to exercise our free will to obey him and live a life worthy of him. As the Christian depends on Jesus' authority, the Christian Disciple gains wisdom, guidance, and power. As we receive his love and grace, we are to show his love and grace to others.

You go

If Jesus had not risen from the dead, then his Disciples would not have had a story to tell. But Jesus had indeed risen from the dead, and the early Church exploded numerically as the twelve

Disciples exercised Jesus' authority and his power.

We read about the growth of the early Church in the Book of Acts in the Bible. Christianity is a faith whereby all Christian Disciples – all followers of Jesus - are to tell others of the goodness of God. Indeed, God himself is a missionary God. Ever since Genesis 3 and the fall of man, God has been on a mission to bring and call people back to himself. That was the purpose of the nation of Israel, to be a light to all nations of the goodness and glory of God. That was the purpose when God, who is outside of time and space, entered human history taking on human flesh and restricted himself in a human body as the man we know as Jesus Christ. Jesus' whole mission was one of calling people back to life in God.

As followers of Jesus Christ, all Christian Disciples are to evangelize. Evangelism is showing and telling others of God's message of reconciliation to all people of all time. It is not forcing people to adopt Church standards (1 Corinthians 5:12) and nor is it simply a message of join the Church as a symbol of good works (Ephesians 2:8-10). If people know you are a Christian, they will be watching how you behave, conduct yourself in your life and your words. You are a witness for God – whether you want to be or not. Let's be good witnesses.

The Holy Spirit is coming

How was this all achieved in the 1ˢᵗ century, at the birth of the Jesus' Church? Throughout his ministry, Jesus had talked about how after he was to depart, and that the Holy Spirit would come (John 15:26). It was through the work of the Holy Spirit who was to come upon them, as promised by Jesus after he had ascended back to the right hand of the Father. The Holy Spirit changed them from living in fear to living out their faith boldly! They had great confidence in their God, knowing that through his death and resurrection, Jesus had conquered all enemies.

9. Goings and Comings

[6] So when the apostles were with Jesus, they kept asking him, "Lord, has the time come for you to free Israel and restore our kingdom?"
[7] He replied, "The Father alone has the authority to set those dates and times, and they are not for you to know. [8] But you will receive power when the Holy Spirit comes upon you. And you will be my witnesses, telling people about me everywhere—in Jerusalem, throughout Judea, in Samaria, and to the ends of the earth."
[9] After saying this, he was taken up into a cloud while they were watching, and they could no longer see him. [10] As they strained to see him rising into heaven, two white-robed men suddenly stood among them. [11] "Men of Galilee," they said, "why are you standing here staring into heaven? Jesus has been taken from you into heaven, but someday he will return from heaven in the same way you saw him go!" (Acts 1:6-11)

Jesus Ascends

Jesus has been raised from the dead! What happened next? In this brief series called Consequences, we shall look together at 7 consequences of Jesus' death and resurrection and some of the theological implications.

Jesus' resurrection is the catalyst for the mission of the Church, beginning with the disciples and throughout history. Indeed, the growth and spread of the Church, is a proof of the historical fact of Jesus' physical resurrection or rising from the dead. Having been raised from the dead, Jesus' mission to earth is coming to an end and shortly he will be returning to the right hand of the Father. Just as he had said to his disciples a few times before he went to the Cross. Before he does leave though, he has some final instructions for his disciples.

In the Gospel of Mark 16:14-19, the Gospel of Luke 24:50-51 and from Acts 1:1-12, we read about Jesus physically ascending into the heavens. Jesus has returned to the right hand of the Father, just as he said he would before his death on the Cross.

During their last discussion with Jesus, the disciples were still expecting him to lead a revolution against the Romans (Acts 1:6). Despite all Jesus had said to them in the previous 3 years, they still did not understand that Jesus had come to lead a spiritual kingdom and not a political kingdom. Now it would be easy to think that Jesus has abandoned them, but no! Jesus tells them to go back to Jerusalem, wait for the Holy Spirit and then go tell others the Good News about Him! he had told them previously that he was going away and that it was better for them if he did, because the Holy Spirit would be sent to be with them, to live in them and empower them for the work they had to do!

Even after Jesus had vanished into the clouds, the disciples still gathered around looking into the sky for him to return! So two angels came and say:

"Why are you standing here staring into heaven? Jesus has been taken from you into heaven, but someday he will return from heaven in the same way you saw him go!" (Acts 1:11)

From there the disciples returned to Jerusalem and waited. They didn't have to wait long, 10 days. Who where they waiting for>?

The Holy Spirit Comes

[1] On the day of Pentecost all the believers were meeting together in one place. [2] Suddenly, there was a sound from heaven like the roaring of a

mighty windstorm, and it filled the house where they were sitting. ³ Then, what looked like flames or tongues of fire appeared and settled on each of them. ⁴ And everyone present was filled with the Holy Spirit and began speaking in other languages, as the Holy Spirit gave them this ability.

(Acts 2:1-4)

Jesus has ascended back to the right hand of the Father. The 12 apostles are now back in Jerusalem and waiting. Waiting for the Holy Spirit to come and baptize, fill, empower, indwell and transform. Before Jesus went to the Cross, he told his disciples a number of times that he was going back to the Father, that he would not leave them alone and powerless because the Comforter, the Holy Spirit, would be sent. The Holy Spirit would live in, empower and motivate the disciples. He would also remind them of all Jesus had taught them.

Throughout the Book of Acts and in the other New Testament writings we discover more about the Holy Spirit. We see that his prime role is to see Jesus Christ the Son of God praised and glorified (John 16:13-14) by testifying for Jesus Christ (John 15:26) and witnessing for him (Acts 1:8). The Holy Spirit is involved with ministering to members of the Church. The Holy Spirit declares God's Word, interpreting and illuminating it. He convicts of sin, transforms, indwells, fills, baptizes and seals the believer. With all this, the Holy Spirit also equips for service. God is at work in his body the Church, to will and to act accordingly to his purpose (Phil. 2:13), to be my witnesses (Acts 1:8).

We see evidence of the Holy Spirit at work here, particularly his work in the life of Peter! Remember how Peter had rejected Jesus Christ and openly defied him by trying to stop Jesus going to the Cross. That Peter was a dejected and defeated man. There is now a new Peter! A new Peter who has been utterly transformed by the Holy Spirit! A Peter who speaks with the authority Jesus gave all the disciples. This Peter, given impetus by the Holy Spirit, preaches a sermon and 3000 people are added to the Church in one day (Acts 2:41). This Peter, who when passing by a man who couldn't walk, told him to get up and walk – and the man did (Acts 3:1-11)! Peter was allowing himself to be guided and controlled by the Holy Spirit. The difference between this Peter and the dejected Peter before Jesus' resurrection is due only to the Holy Spirit making a difference to Peter. Peter, by submitting himself to the authority and power of the Holy Spirit, was allowing the Holy Spirit to control him and guide him. The greatest evidence of the Holy Spirit living inside any of us, is the transformation of the individual into the image of Jesus – as demonstrated here in Peter.

This Peter who under the influence of Holy Spirit's power, administered Church discipline as in the case of Ananias and Sapphira (Acts 5:10). But it wasn't just Peter who was empowered. As Acts 5:12-16 shows us, all the disciples, not just the twelve apostles, were able to do all manner of things for the glory of Jesus Christ because they were baptized and controlled by the Holy Spirit.

The Holy Spirit empowers and delivers the disciples passion for making Jesus Christ known. The early Church was dynamic and seen to be exercising the authority of Jesus Christ. This was done by preaching the good news about Jesus being the long waited for Messiah. The Disciples exercised Jesus' authority by submitting themselves to and relying upon the Holy Spirit. Would that be for the Church of the 21st century? The Holy Spirit lives inside and empowers all believers for the service and glory of Jesus Christ!

10. Cross Purposes

[42] So Jesus called them together and said, "You know that the rulers in this world lord it over their people, and officials flaunt their authority over those under them. [43] But among you it will be different. Whoever wants to be a leader among you must be your servant, [44] and whoever wants to be first among you must be the slave of everyone else. [45] For even the Son of Man came not to be served but to serve others and to give his life as a ransom for many."
(Mark 10:42-45)

[16] "For this is how God loved the world: he gave his one and only Son, so that everyone who believes in him will not perish but have eternal life. [17] God sent his Son into the world not to judge the world, but to save the world through Him.
(John 3:16-17)

Even a superficial look at the media today, will tell you that the world we live in is messed up and it seems to be getting even worse! Is there any hope? Yes, indeed there is! That is why God sent Jesus. Jesus is the hope. Jesus came to serve rather than be served. That is why Jesus came to give his life, so humanity may have a hope. God made the world perfect and humanity was in a harmonious relationship with God. Humanity messed it up and broke the relationship bonds with God. When the time was right, God became human, in order to bring humanity back into relationship with himself. Without Jesus' death on the Cross, there would be no hope for the world. That he died is without doubt. But why did he have to die and so what?

God's Character

By his very nature, God is loving and compassionate, forgiving, faithful and slow to anger - Exodus 34:6-7. That is the part we are most comfortable with, if we are honest. Yet God is holy, righteous and just. Therefore, God must punish sin because that is part of his nature as well. That is the part we as 21st century people are most uncomfortable with. We love to think of God as being all soft, loving and gentle. We don't like to think of him as a Judge who must punish sin.

When we think like that though, we forget that God loves righteousness and hates wickedness (Psalm 45:7). Therefore, sin must be dealt with and it cannot simply be ignored. God is set apart from humanity and holy, and if he wasn't, he would not be worthy of being worshipped. If God were like that, then he would be part of the problem. So, how can God be both a holy, righteous God and accept sinners? he does this by declaring sinners righteous. But why and how does he do this? Where do humans fit into the picture?

Humanity's sin

Sin is what separates humans from God and is anything that separates humanity from God. As a consequence, this leads to both a spiritual and physical death (Romans 3:23, Romans 6:23, Isaiah 59:2). and consequently leads to both a spiritual and physical death.

Such as expressed by the Old Testament Prophet, Isaiah:

[1] Listen! The LORD's arm is not too weak to save you, nor is his ear too deaf to hear you call.
[2] It's your sins that have cut you off from God. Because of your sins, he has turned away and will not listen anymore.
(Isaiah 59:1-2)

Paul also expressly states this fact in his letter to the 1st century Church in Rome:

> 22 But now you are free from the power of sin and have become slaves of God. Now you do those things that lead to holiness and result in eternal life. 23 For the wages of sin is death, but the free gift of God is eternal life through Christ Jesus our Lord.
>
> (Romans 6:22-23)

Nobody escapes this condemnation as all have sinned and fallen short of the glory of God.

> 23 For everyone has sinned; we all fall short of God's glorious standard.
>
> (Romans 3:23)

The problem!

Sin as described in the Bible, is the lack of conformity to the Moral Law of God, either in deeds, attitudes, or state. Jesus' close friend John, reflected on it later in his life, when he wrote:

> "Everyone who sins breaks the law; in fact, sin is lawlessness."
>
> (1 John 3:4)

Jesus during his public ministry, said that the two greatest commands were to love God and love all others as you would love yourself (Mark 12:30-31))? Any breakage of those two commandments is sin, whether by a little or a lot. Yet, there are two kinds of sin. Firstly, there are the sins, which are active disobedience of a known will, law or commandment of God. These are sins of commission.

Secondly, there are the passive sins, where something that should be done, is not done. These are sins of omission which occur when people are not doing as they ought to do (James 4:17).

The solution

In the Old Testament, sins were dealt with by blood sacrifices of atonement as coverings for sin (Leviticus 17:11), for without the shedding of blood there can be no forgiveness (Hebrews 9:22). A blood sacrifice was God's way of dealing with sin and they signified several things:

- That a gracious God was prepared to overlook the sin of the repentant person
- Visually it provided a covering for sin.
- It showed the great cost of sin.
- It was an exchange or substitution.
- It was only always going to be a temporary measure as it pointed forward to the death of Jesus.

Under the Old Testament Law or Covenant, sins were dealt with by blood sacrifices of atonement for sin (Leviticus 17:11)[1]. The writer to the New Testament letter to the Hebrews stipulates that without the shedding of blood, there can be no remission of sin (Hebrews 9:22). A blood sacrifice was God's way of dealing with sin.

These blood sacrifices of the Old Testament signified several things:
- They provided a covering for sin.
- They showed the great cost of sin.
- They were an exchange or substitution.
- They were only always going to be a temporary measure as they pointed forward to Jesus' sacrificial death on the Cross.

However, the ultimate solution to sin was not the continual animal sacrifice of the Old Testament because the blood of animals was unable take away sin because they were only a veneer. That was why it was necessary to repeat time and time again! But those animal sacrifices pointed forward to a time when they would no longer be necessary! They pointed forward to the time when only through the Christ's death on the Cross, that sin would be taken

---

[1] We look at this in more detail in Appendix 2: Assured Atonement

away (Hebrews 9:11-15, 26-28) and not merely covered or coated! You may well ask now, as other have done for the last 2000 years: "What has all this to do with Jesus?" We see throughout the Gospels how Jesus Christ was tempted and taunted by satan to disobey God to the extent of not going to his death on the Cross. If Jesus had ever succumbed to temptation, and sinned against God in thought, word, action or inaction, then he himself would have needed a Saviour. That is why Jesus is the perfect sacrifice – because he never sinned, and he always did what he saw God the Father wanting him to do. Because of the Cross and resurrection alone, satan, death and sin have all lost their sting and have been vanquished. WOW!

Substitution

Jesus died for our sin, the righteous for the unrighteous (1 Peter 3:18). That is how God can be both a holy, righteous God and accept sinners. That is why Jesus needed to be both fully God and fully human. If he had not been either, it would not have been the full substitutionary sacrifice that was necessary to bear the permanent consequences of sin. Because he was God, his sacrifice was sufficient. Because he was also man, he could die in our place. While we were still sinners Christ died for us, (Romans 5:6-8), willingly giving his life as a ransom for many (Mark 10:45) and when he died in our place on the Cross, he bore the consequences of all sin – past, present and future.

This substitution was the sacrifice, or sin offering, required in order that Jesus as the Lamb of God could take away the sins of the world (John 1:29). He became sin for us (2 Corinthians 5:21) and it was his precious blood as a lamb without blemish or defect (1 Peter 1:18-19) that fulfils God's requirements permanently. He was the propitiation for all sin turning away the wrath of God from all those prepared to accept his work on their behalf.

Propitiation

I often hear things like, God is love, so I don't have to worry about my own lifestyle or my morals, because God is love. When I die, he will accept me simply because I have tried my best. And of course, that is partly true. God is indeed a God of love. But we must also remember that towards sin and sinful behaviour, he has great fury, anger and wrath. Look at these statements by Paul:

> [18] But God shows his anger from heaven against all sinful, wicked people who suppress the truth by their wickedness. [19] They know the truth

about God because he has made it obvious to them. [20] For ever since the world was created, people have seen the earth and sky. Through everything God made, they can clearly see his invisible qualities—his eternal power and divine nature. So they have no excuse for not knowing God.

[21] Yes, they knew God, but they wouldn't worship him as God or even give him thanks. And they began to think up foolish ideas of what God was like. As a result, their minds became dark and confused.

[22] Claiming to be wise, they instead became utter fools. [23] And instead of worshiping the glorious, ever-living God, they worshiped idols made to look like mere people and birds and animals and reptiles. [24] So God abandoned them to do whatever shameful things their hearts desired. As a result, they did vile and degrading things with each other's bodies. [25] They traded the truth about God for a lie. So they worshiped and served the things God created instead of the Creator himself, who is worthy of eternal praise! Amen.

(Romans 1:18-25)

The emphasis here is being thrown back on to the effects on human beings of their conduct, but the general tone is that God is against sin. Nothing we say or do can appease his hatred of sin and sinful lifestyles. Nothing we can do is able to appease God's anger, because his anger toward sin is unquenchable. Unquenchable that is, except for one thing!

This word, propitiation, basically means the turning aside of anger, in this context of God's anger by the sacrifice of Jesus Christ. All God's anger and judgment of sin falls on Jesus Christ, instead of on us. But in order to accept the effect of that for yourself, you need to ask God to accept the sacrifice of Jesus on your behalf in order to appease his anger towards your sin (Isaiah 53:5; Romans 3:25; 1 John 2:2).

Jesus was the sacrifice of atonement[2], or propitiation, as the one who would quench God's anger towards sinful people, by taking away sin through his death on the Cross. This shows Jesus as being both the just one and the one who justifies. (Romans 3:25-26, see the sections on Sacrifice and Jesus' Cross) Only through him could the sins of the whole world, past, present and future, be forgiven.

---

[2] Atonement means *'at–one–ment'*, which is a bringing together of an offended party and the offender to be as one, so not too different from propitiation.

To some people, even some in the Church, this is abhorrent. The very thought that God could willing send his son to be a blood sacrifice for sin is tantamount to abuse, some say. However, God's requirements are very clear. John 3:16 says it is all part of the grand scheme of redemption:

> [16] "For this is how God loved the world: he gave [his] one and only Son, so that everyone who believes in him will not perish but have eternal life. [17] God sent his Son into the world not to judge the world, but to save the world through him.
> (John 3:16-17)

If there was any other way, would not God have done it that way? As a Christian, live a life that is holy and pleasing to God. Not to somehow pave your own way into heaven, for that is already assured by way of Jesus' death on the Cross. Remember no sacrifice you make is greater than the one God has already made by sending his Son to death as a propitiation for your sin, (1 John 4:10). This shows God's real love. It is a love which is a tough yet all-embracing Love.

The Cross is a choice

And there is yet more to the Cross and

resurrection of Jesus Christ! All human beings, in their natural state, are born sinners and have rebelled against God (Romans 3:23). However, because of Jesus' death on the Cross, God offers forgiveness (Ephesians 1:7), peace (Romans 5:1) and reconciliation (2 Corinthians 5:19). Through the Cross, humanity can choose to be made just before God (Romans 3:24-26) as it cleanses from sin (1 John 1:7) and declares humanity right before Almighty God (2 Corinthians 5:21).

Because of the Cross, humanity can choose to have direct access to God (Ephesians 2:18) and Jesus Christ intercedes for them (Hebrews 2:17-18). Because of Jesus Christ's death on the Cross and his resurrection, all those who choose to follow him have freedom from slavery to sin (Galatians 5:1) and freedom from the power of the devil (Hebrews 2:14). None of the above things are true if a person is not a follower of Jesus Christ.

Ultimately the Cross and resurrection brings you to a choice. You can accept the Cross and therefore be guaranteed peace with God. The Cross of Jesus Christ and his resurrection epitomises God's glory. Jesus Christ, as the Son of God who is outside of time and space, entered the time and space of this world and became human. He died on a Cross, taking on himself the sins of the world, paying the greatest price, so that humanity can choose to be restored back into a peaceful relationship with God the Father. That is for all people, of all nations, ages, generations, statuses and gender. There is a price to pay for those seeking to be followers of Jesus Christ! They must surrender completely to him, be prepared to identify with him in suffering and death and be willing to follow him obediently, wherever he leads.

Jesus death on the Cross was preached by the early Church! That is also to be our message as Church in the 21st century, but that was only part of their message!

Significance of the Resurrection

But if it is preached that Christ has been raised from the dead, how can some of you say that there is no resurrection of the dead? If there is no resurrection of the dead, then not even Christ has been raised. And if Christ has not been raised, our preaching is useless and so is your faith.
(1 Corinthians 15:12-14)

That was the Apostle Paul, writing to the Corinthian Church about the crucified Jesus having been physically raised from the dead! What significance is there in Jesus' resurrection, that the early Church afforded such great value in it as part of their message? The resurrection of Jesus Christ provided the central theme for the sermons and teaching in the early Church (Acts 1:22; Acts 4:33, Acts 17:18). Certainly within 'Paul-ine' theology, but what significance is there in Jesus' resurrection?

The resurrection proved and vindicated all of Jesus' teaching and claims as the suffering Servant and attested to his being fully God, fully human and the last Judge of all mankind (Isaiah 53:10-12; Acts 2:36; Acts 3:13-15; Romans 1:4). The resurrection declared God's approval of Jesus' obedient service and the fulfilment of Old Testament promises as well as Jesus' own words about it! The Cross and resurrection of Jesus results in forgiveness of sins and salvation being only found in and through Jesus Christ.

This was the prime motive for evangelism in the early Church (Acts 2:32, Romans 4:24-25). Jesus' resurrection is a sign of the bodily resurrection for all believers in him, giving a new attitude to death and transforming hopes (Romans 8:10, 1 Corinthians 15:12-58, 2 Corinthians 4:14; 1 Peter 1:3 & 21). As the resurrected King, Jesus now intercedes for us and has perfected the redemption of all those who choose to follow him (Romans 5:10; Hebrews 6:20, 1 Peter 1:21).

Finally the Cross and resurrection ensure victory over satan, sin and death – they are conquered and squashed. Satan is a defeated creature and will do anything to drag people into defeat with him. The power of sin is conquered, and sin's grip is overcome if you are a believer in Jesus Christ. Finally, death has been vanquished, because all those who believe and trust in Jesus Christ will live forever with him. Therefore for the believer, death is not the end but a beginning. If Jesus Christ did not physically rise from the dead, we as Christians are the product of the greatest delusional lie and are the most foolish of all people.

Resurrection of Christians

Jesus' resurrection is the guarantee that all humans will be resurrected (1 Corinthians 15:20-22). Amazing love. There will be a bodily resurrection of the dead, those who are saved and those who are unsaved (John 5:28-29; Acts 24:15). What will our resurrected bodies be like?

We get a good glimpse from the Bible writers, particularly in the New Testament. We see that the resurrected body of believers, all those who are truly disciples of Jesus Christ, will be:

- Like Christ's glorious body (1 Corinthians 15:49; Philippians 3:21; 1 John 3:2)

- Not just flesh and blood (1 Corinthians 15:50ff)
- Not just spiritual (Luke 24:39; 1 Corinthians 15:42, 53)

Those who are, or were, non-believers will also be resurrected (John 5:28-29), but will not have the new glorious bodies of believers, nor will they enter into heaven. Instead they will be cast into darkness. It makes the work of evangelism for all Christians, all the more imperative.

Ultimately Jesus gives all humanity a choice. You can choose to deny his Cross and resurrection of Jesus Christ and say it doesn't matter. You can say that it is an irrelevance and that is your right. God's love is compelling and amazing, but he does not force anyone to love him in return, because love never forces! Such is the enormity of the love of God that each person has a choice to make – follow Jesus and accept his Cross and resurrection or not to do that. God will not force you to accept it, but he will keep on calling you back to the Cross and resurrection of Jesus.

Jesus death on the Cross and his resurrection was the central message of the early Church and should be central to the message of the Church today and tomorrow!

11. Response Required

[6] We know what real love is because Jesus gave up his life for us. So we also ought to give up our lives for our brothers and sisters. (1 John 3:16)

Now a question. What is our response to the events of Easter to be? Our first response if we are followers of Jesus is that we are to love. Love not just in words but also in action. Love God and love others. What kind of love? It is to be a practical, self-less, giving and sacrificial love.

Jesus told all his followers to take up their Cross if they were to follow him as his Disciple. What does this mean? Jesus said these words:

23 Then he said to the crowd, "If any of you wants to be my follower, you must give up your own way, take up your Cross daily, and follow me. 24 If you try to hang on to your life, you will lose it. But if you give up your life for my sake, you will save it. 25 And what do you benefit if you gain the whole world but are yourself lost or destroyed? 26 If anyone is ashamed of me and my message, the Son of Man will be ashamed of that person when he returns in his glory and in the glory of the Father and the holy angels. (Luke 9:23-26)

What does this phrase "carry a cross" mean? At that time in history, it must have been just about the most degrading thing you could possibly ask anyone to do in those days. And not only degrading, also incredibly painful as it would have followed a terrible scourging and been followed by the most terrible death. Did he really mean what he said? It seems so because the record suggests that Peter died just that way. The apostle James had it easy – he was just beheaded! (Acts 12:2)

What is our response to that to be? It must be just about the hardest, toughest, most difficult thing Jesus ever said to his followers. We are being commanded to count the cost of following him. That is how we carry our own Cross for the sake of Jesus Christ. Jesus wants to be number one in the life of all those who choose to follow him. Jesus wants supremacy over everything in our lives, including family, friends, and possessions. Alas, that's a cost too high for some.

Here is one man who couldn't give up something to follow Jesus: let's call him Basil. Basil runs up to Jesus and wants eternal life, wants it now and asks Jesus about how to get it. He has fully kept the commandments listed by Jesus. However, when Jesus said to Basil that to follow him, he would have to give up all his wealth and possessions in order to have treasure in heaven and eternal life, Basil leaves disconsolate and shattered. The life of Basil, this rich young ruler, reflected a life of absorption with his own self-interest and self-importance.

It was a step too far for Basil. He wanted his riches and also everlasting life, but Jesus said that he couldn't have both. He remains the only person that we know of, who left Jesus' presence sorrowful. That was due to Basil putting his trust in himself, his riches and his wealth alone. Now riches, in and of themselves, are not necessarily wrong. But for Basil, well, he was not willing to make the sacrifice required to follow Jesus. He couldn't count the cost of following Jesus– it was too high a price for him to pay (Matthew 19:16-25).

What have you given up as a result of your decision to follow Jesus? Making sacrifices to follow Jesus is all part of the WOW factor of Jesus. Jesus demands that he be number one and supreme over everything else in your life - yourself, family, others and material goods including money and possessions. How is this to be done? By constantly ensuring that your works and words match your lifestyle and that no hypocrisy can be found or will be found in your life. It means standing up for God in the face of adversity. It means loving others even though they hate you.

Just a couple of examples: In the UK, we aren't systematically persecuted; we are marginalized, ridiculed and ignored. In some other parts of the world members of our Christian family daily face death simply because they chose to follow Jesus. They are carrying their Cross for Jesus.

What about us? For example, if we as

Christians were known by our self-sacrificial love of all others, then Jesus whom we claim to love, follow, worship, and adore would be seen. The Christian is a person who has taken up their own Cross in following Jesus and count the cost of being a disciple of Jesus Christ.

As we have seen, Jesus told us to take up our own Cross if we are to follow him as his Disciple. How is that possible? If we try to do that in our own strength and wisdom, we will fail. If we do it using the power and strength of the Holy Spirit within us, then we will succeed at following Jesus' command. Are you as a Disciple of Jesus Christ willing to take up your Cross and follow him? What a difference that would make to the community where you live.

There is a price to pay for being a true follower of Jesus Christ! Followers are to surrender completely to him in all aspects of life! Followers identify with him in suffering and death and follow him obediently, wherever he leads. Followers are to take up their own Cross in order to show that they are followers of Jesus Christ – the King of Kings and Lord of Lords.

The Cross is a choice

The Cross is God's solution to the suffering, evil, troubles and sin of the world. Only by Jesus Christ going to the Cross have evil, sin, suffering and satan been dealt mortal blows. The Cross provides the victorious solution. The Cross is not a symbol to be merely placed around the neck on a chain, to be worn as a lapel pin, or as an item statement of fashion. The Cross is not meant to portray Jesus as some form of sadomasochistic 'tragi-hero' as some people try to make it out to be. The Cross is God's solution to the problem of evil, sin, suffering and pain, as much as the wise of this world would love to think that it is not.

The Cross is a choice. You can choose to deny the Cross and say it doesn't matter. You can say that it is an irrelevance and that is your right. God will not force you to accept the Cross and love him. If he did, he would have created Adam so that Adam would automatically love him and not given Adam free will to rebel. That way the Cross would not have been needed.

But such is the enormity of the love of God, that each person, including you and I, have a choice to make – follow Jesus and take up your own Cross and be an overcomer for him. God will not force you to accept it, but he will keep on calling you back to the Cross. It is his initiative. Calling sometimes in quiet ways and at other times, much more loudly. You can deny the Cross and its meaning and when Jesus Christ comes again in judgment, you will find that he denies you entrance into his glorious kingdom. When Jesus comes again, everyone will know who he is and bow down to him. But only those whom he knows, will be granted access into everlasting life.

How you think of the Cross, ultimately has relevance to you and affects your reality. You can accept the Cross as your personal substitution, personal propitiation and personal redemption. That way you have peace with God. The Cross of Jesus Christ thoroughly epitomises God's glory, and if there were any other way that God the Father could restore people into relationship with himself, then surely, he would have done it that way.

But there was no other way – Jesus Christ, as the Son of God who was simultaneously fully God and fully human, died on a Roman Cross. He took on the sins of the world, paying the greatest price, so that you can be restored into a peaceful relationship with God the Father. That is for all people, of all nations, ages, generations, statuses and gender.

The Cross is amazing love in action and is ignored at great peril. Let us go forward in hope and faith, choosing deliberately not to boast in anything else, save only of Jesus Christ and him crucified. The wisdom of God as exhibited on and in the Cross of Jesus Christ, is foolishness but only to those who don't accept it.

But it is more than that for the Christian! For example if we as Christians were known by our self-sacrificial love of all others, then Jesus whom we claim to love, follow, worship, and adore would be seen. When Jesus calls a person to follow him, he calls them to a life which is utterly and totally devoted to him. He calls the Christian to die to self and to live for God alone. It is no offer that a person makes to Jesus, but rather the call that Jesus puts upon the person. He calls Christians to a live totally devoted to him, a life of intimacy with him. The Christian is a person has taken up their own Cross in following Jesus and count the cost of being a disciple of Jesus Christ.

Jesus still meets people today

To those that have responded to Jesus and are following him, Jesus still meets with them. How does he do this?

Jesus walks with us, wherever we go and in particular in the darkest periods of our life. Just as he did with the two people on the road to Emmaus, he walks with those who proclaim to follow him (Mark 16:12-13, Luke 24:13-32).

Jesus speaks whenever the Bible is faithfully preached and read from, just as he opened the eyes of those on the Emmaus road when he explained the Scriptures (Luke 24:27). Jesus meets us in the Communion or Lord's Supper, with the bread and wine, which symbolise his flesh and blood as an act of remembrance of what he did for humanity. Because of Jesus' physical resurrection from the dead, it symbolises and shows that we as Christians have also risen from the dead! Our old nature is dead, and our new nature is alive! In the sacrament of baptism, Christ's death is symbolised in our going under the water bodily, just as his resurrection is symbolised when we are raised up and out of the water! WOW! Jesus Christ – dead, buried and raised to new life! The Christian – dies to self, buries their old sinful nature and raised to new life in Jesus Christ with a new nature, ready to serve the risen Jesus! WOW!

More than that, his resurrection was not merely coming back to life. Jesus had raised people back to life during his ministry. But those people would go on to die again. Jesus was not like that, because he had new and glorious body!   And we too will one day have new bodies! WOW!

If you are not yet a follower of this Jesus, then start following now! You may not have another opportunity to do so!

12. What Is Easter All About?

[42] So Jesus called them together and said, "You know that the rulers in this world lord it over their people, and officials flaunt their authority over those under them. [43] But among you it will be different. Whoever wants to be a leader among you must be your servant, [44] and whoever wants to be first among you must be the slave of everyone else. [45] For even the Son of Man came not to be served but to serve others and to give his life as a ransom for many." (Mark 10:42-45)

As we have seen, there is a problem in the world, which has been a problem since time almost began! That problem is sin, disobedience against God. Sin is anything that separates humans from God, which as a consequence leads to both a spiritual and physical death (Romans 3:23, Romans 6:23, Isaiah 59:2). Under the Old Testament Law or Covenant, sins were dealt with by blood sacrifices of atonement for sin (Leviticus 17:11), for without the shedding of blood there can be no remission of sin (Hebrews 9:22). A blood sacrifice was God's way of dealing with sin. These blood sacrifices of the Old Testament signified several things:

- They provided a covering for sin.
- They showed the great cost of sin.
- They were an exchange or substitution.
- They were only always going to be a temporary measure as they pointed forward to Jesus' sacrificial death on the Cross.

However, the ultimate solution to sin was not the continual animal sacrifice of the Old Testament because the blood of animals was unable take away sin because they were only a veneer. That was why it was necessary to repeat time and time again! But those animal sacrifices pointed forward to a time when they would no longer be necessary! They pointed forward to the time when only through the Christ's death on the Cross, that sin would be taken away (Hebrews 9:11-15, 26-28) and not merely covered or coated!

What has this to do with Jesus? We see in the Gospels how Jesus Christ was tempted and taunted by satan to disobey God to the extent of not going to his death on the Cross. If Jesus had ever succumbed to temptation, and sinned against God in thought, word, action or inaction, then he himself would have needed a Saviour. That is why Jesus is the perfect sacrifice – because he never sinned, and he always did what he saw God the Father wanting him to do. Because of the Cross and resurrection alone, satan, death and sin have all lost their sting and have been vanquished. WOW!

The Cross is a Choice

And there is yet more to the Cross and resurrection of Jesus Christ! All human beings, in their natural state, are born sinners and have rebelled against God (Romans 3:23). However, because of Jesus' death on the Cross, God offers forgiveness (Ephesians 1:7), peace (Romans 5:1) and reconciliation (2 Corinthians 5:19). Through the Cross, humanity can choose to be made just before God (Romans 3:24-26) as it cleanses from sin (1 John

1:7) and declares humanity right before Almighty God (2 Corinthians 5:21). Because of the Cross, humanity can choose to have direct access to God (Ephesians 2:18) and Jesus Christ intercedes for them (Hebrews 2:17-18). Because of Jesus Christ's death on the Cross and his resurrection, all those who choose to follow him have freedom from slavery to sin (Galatians 5:1) and freedom from the power of the devil (Hebrews 2:14). None of the above things are true if a person is not a follower of Jesus Christ.

Ultimately the Cross and resurrection brings you to a choice. You can accept the Cross and therefore be guaranteed peace with God. The Cross of Jesus Christ and his resurrection epitomises God's glory. Jesus Christ, as the Son of God who is outside of time and space, entered the time and space of this world and became human. He died on a Cross, taking on himself the sins of the world, paying the greatest price, so that humanity can choose to be restored back into a peaceful relationship with God the Father. That is for all people, of all nations, ages, generations, statuses and gender. There is a price to pay for those seeking to be followers of Jesus Christ! They must surrender completely to him, be prepared to identify with him in suffering and death and be willing to follow him obediently, wherever he leads. Jesus death on the Cross was preached by the early Church! That is also to be our message as Church in the 21st century, but that was only part of their message, as we will now go on to see.

Significance of the Resurrection

> But if it is preached that Christ has been raised from the dead, how can some of you say that there is no resurrection of the dead? If there is no resurrection of the dead, then not even Christ has been raised. And if Christ has not been raised, our preaching is useless and so is your faith.
> (1 Corinthians 15:12-14)

That was the Apostle Paul, writing to the Corinthian Church about the crucified Jesus having been physically raised from the dead! What significance is there in Jesus' resurrection, that the early Church afforded such great value in it as part of their message? The resurrection of Jesus Christ provided the central theme for the sermons and teaching in the early Church (Acts 1:22; Acts 4:33, Acts 17:18). Certainly within 'Paul-ine' theology, but what significance is there in Jesus' resurrection?

The resurrection proved and vindicated all of Jesus' teaching and claims as the suffering Servant and attested to his being fully God, fully human and the last Judge of all mankind (Isaiah 53:10-12; Acts 2:36; Acts 3:13-15; Romans 1:4). The resurrection declared God's approval of Jesus' obedient service and the fulfilment of Old Testament promises as well as Jesus' own words about it!

The Cross and resurrection of Jesus results in forgiveness of sins and salvation being only found in and through Jesus Christ. This was the prime motive for evangelism in the early Church (Acts 2:32, Romans 4:24-25). Jesus' resurrection is a sign of the bodily resurrection for all believers in him, giving a new attitude to death and transforming hopes (1 Corinthians 15:12-58, Romans 8:10, 2 Corinthians 4:14; 1 Peter 1:3 & 21). As the resurrected King, Jesus now intercedes for us and has perfected the redemption of all those who choose to follow him (Romans 5:10; Hebrews 6:20, 1 Peter 1:21).

Finally the Cross and resurrection ensure victory over satan, sin and death – they are conquered and squashed. Satan is a defeated creature and will do anything to drag people into defeat with him. The power of sin is conquered, and sin's grip is overcome if you are a believer in Jesus Christ. Finally, as I said earlier, death has been beaten, because those who believe and trust in

Jesus Christ will live forever with him – death is not the end but a beginning. if Jesus Christ did not physically rise from the dead, we as Christians are the product of the greatest delusional lie and are the most foolish of all people.

Resurrection of Christians

Jesus' resurrection is the guarantee that all humans will be resurrected (1 Corinthians 15:20-22). Amazing love. There will be a bodily resurrection of the dead, those who are saved and those who are unsaved (John 5:28-29; Acts 24:15). What will our resurrected bodies be like? We get a good glimpse from the Bible writers. The resurrected body of believers, those who are truly disciples of Jesus Christ will be:

- Like Christ's glorious body (1 Corinthians 15:49; Philippians 3:21; 1 John 3:2)
- Not just flesh and blood (1 Corinthians 15:50ff)
- Not just spiritual (Luke 24:39; 1 Corinthians 15:42, 53)

Those who are, or were, non-believers will also be resurrected (John 5:28-29), but will not have the new glorious bodies of believers, nor will they enter into heaven. Instead they will be cast into darkness.

It makes the work of evangelism for all Christians, all the more imperative.

Ultimately Jesus gives all humanity a choice. You can choose to deny his Cross and resurrection of Jesus Christ and say it doesn't matter. You can say that it is an irrelevance and that is your right. God's love is compelling and amazing, but he does not force anyone to love him in return, because love never forces! Such is the enormity of the love of God that each person has a choice to make – follow Jesus and accept his Cross and resurrection or not to do that. God will not force you to accept it, but he will keep on calling you back to the Cross and resurrection of Jesus. It is then, when you can have true forgiveness from God, be justified before God by God and have true peace with and from God.

Justified

As an additional consequence of Jesus' death on the cross, Christians are justified before God and by God. That means that God regards you as if you have never sinned against him. He has declared you to be righteous (even if you are not). That means you are declared free from the penalty of your sin and at the final judgement to come, you will be considered righteous and accepted by God on the basis of the completed work of Jesus on the

Cross. Justification is only a reality to you, if you have taken up the offer and are a follower of Jesus Christ.

The basis of this justification is that God is both the Just and the Justifier of sinners (Romans 3:21-26). God is holy; therefore, sin must be dealt with. He is just so he cannot arbitrarily forgive sin. However. he can do so because the judgment and penalty of sin, which is death, was poured out on Jesus Christ who is the substitute for all sinners.

Therefore. justice has been done, and therefore God is just, even although he has justified sinners. By faith in Jesus Christ we are declared righteous as a gift, and, as who have committed ourselves as believers in Jesus, are therefore justified. Nothing we could do would make us justified before Almighty God. It is only through His grace this can happen and by no other way. That grace which is freely available to all who take God up on his free offer.

Peace

The world we live in, wants peace. The world is unified around the concept of peace. However, the peace the world wants requires the manipulation of circumstances. God's peace, however, comes regardless of circumstances.

'Shalom' was the Hebrew word used in the Old Testament for our word, 'peace'. It means a wholeness of well-being and mind; the total absence of conflict and turmoil evidenced by an untroubled mind and a heart that does not fear. It is total harmony with God, man, circumstances and self. That is true peace.

As we have seen earlier, this true peace ended when Adam sinned, and fellowship was broken between God and humans. God is a God of peace (1 Thessalonians 5:23). and the Kingdom of God is about peace in the Holy Spirit (Romans 14:17). Jesus is referred to in prophecy as the Prince of Peace, for example in Isaiah 9:6. As a Christian Disciple, you have peace with God through Jesus Christ's death and resurrection. There are three special areas where peace should reign: God, other people and within yourself.

As a Disciple of Jesus Christ, you have peace with God because you are justified by faith. This peace gives you access into God's grace and blessings (Romans 5:1-2). Jesus Christ is the bridge of peace between God and yourself. Peach with God should cause you to really go "WOW!"

Jesus removes the need for all hostility between other people and you, and thus clears the way for peace to reign there too. You are to live at peace with everyone and not to be proud or vengeful

(Romans 12:17-20). Any vengeance that may need to be applied should only come from the Lord. You are to do what is right in the eyes of other people and exhibit positive goodness. You are to make every effort to do what leads to peace and mutual edification (Romans 14:13, 17-19), and not place stumbling blocks in front of others.

As a Disciple of Christ, you have the gift of peace with God, given by the God of peace (Philippians 4:7-9; Colossians 3:15) given to you through Jesus Christ who is the Prince of Peace. (John 14:27). You are to be a peacemaker, generated by having internal peace yourself. This shows the fruit of the Spirit. When faced with troubled times and a troubled world, you can have peace through an untroubled heart and mind clear of fear (John 16:33).

How do we gain peace within? As you live a life in obedience to Jesus, you bear the fruit of righteousness, which is peace, quietness and confidence (Isaiah 32:17). A mind controlled by the Holy Spirit of peace gives a life of peace and total trust in God. (Isaiah 26:3; Romans 8:6). Lastly, when you are content whatever the situation, this enables the peace of God to guard your heart and mind (Philippians 4:11-13). Peace with God, others and yourself because of Easter.

Born Again

Another consequence of Easter and being at peace with God is that Christians are 'born again'. Early in Jesus' ministry, he taught Nicodemus, a Jewish leader a lesson when he said, "I tell you the truth, unless you are born again, you cannot see the Kingdom of God.". This thoroughly confused Nicodemus then, and it confuses some people even today.

Every person that has ever lived has something in common with every other person that has ever lived. They have been born physically. Of course, they only know the time and date of their physical birth, because somebody told them. They also had no say in whether they wanted to be born physically or not. Just as each person has a physical body, each person also has a spirit.

Now the spirit in everybody is our spiritual system, which can be seen in our general conscience, for most people in a consciousness of God, and faith (if we have any). Each person is made up of an outward physical body and an internal spirit. Into this general spiritual side of life can be grafted the Holy Spirit – he is "born" into us. That is why Jesus said that to be one of His followers you had to be "born again". This phrase can also be translated "born from above". That phrase "from above" emphasises that it is something that you cannot do for yourself. It is a direct work of God, borne from his love of you from his wellsprings of grace and mercy, when you are "born again" or "born from above".

To be "born again" you need to say to God you want to be "born again. You need to bow the knee before him and say that you want to dedicate your life to him, that you want to live for Him and that you want to have the Holy Spirit in your life. God will never force you to have the Holy Spirit, but He will keep on calling your name, urging you to come to Him. You may or may not know the exact time and date of when this took place, but be assured, one day your Heavenly Father will tell you.

And what is the result of being "born again"? Having accepted the Father's call to be "born again", you are now: ·

- a new creation (2 Corinthians 5:17)
- a new person created to be like God in true righteousness and holiness in a lifelong process of regeneration. (Ephesians 4:24)
- washed by rebirth and renewal by the Holy Spirit (Titus 3:5)
- now truly alive, not just physically but also now spiritually (Ephesians 2:5)

The events of Easter bring about all these things and it is only through Jesus' death and his resurrection that they can be attained. Attained as an act of grace on God's part, a free gift which is to be opened, in order to be truly received. Jesus death on the Cross and his resurrection was the central message of the early Church! Should that not also be the central message of the Church in the 21st century and beyond until Jesus, who is the Lord of the Church returns to gather those who are His?

Appendix 1: Who was Jesus?

Which Jesus are we talking about here? Is it the Jesus who is a tragi-hero of the stage, the Jesus of the cults, the Jesus of Islam, Hinduism or Buddhism? Let's look a little deeper into which Jesus we are talking about and seeing the real Jesus and not an adapted figure from the imagination of some humans.

The word 'Christ' is the New Testament word for the Old Testament word, Messiah. We look firstly to the Old Testament, in order to understand what the New Testament word Christ means. It was appended to his name in the New Testament, as a way of expressing who he was.

Several of the more recent translations of the New Testament use "Messiah" when it is clearly the office that Jesus filled which is in view and Christ when it is more nearly a name. This is a useful distinction because many people only think of it as the surname, or second name, of Jesus every time it is used.

In the Old Testament, the word translated as 'Messiah' is found only twice (Daniel 9:25-26). The most modern translations have the word as the 'Anointed One'. The Old Testament idea of the word Messiah has five principles attached to it:

- God's chosen and anointed man
- He will bring salvation for God's people
- He will judge God's enemies

- He is an appointed ruler over the nations
- He is an active representative of God

Somewhat surprisingly, these five principles can also be applied to King Cyrus (Isaiah 45:1). Cyrus is an example of an anointed one, a Messiah from God, even though he was not one of God's people, the Israelites. This shows that the word Messiah can also have a non-religious meaning behind it.

The Messiah, God's Anointed One, is pictured in several ways in the Old Testament. There is

- the Suffering Servant (Isaiah 11:1-3; 40-55 and in particular, Isaiah 52:13–53:11)
- the Conquering Warrior (Isaiah 56-66 and in particular, Isaiah 63:1-6)
- the Branch - particularly of David (Jeremiah 23:5,6; Zechariah 3:8)
- Son of Man (Daniel 7)
- Anointed Prince (Daniel 9:25-27)

All of the Old Testament Covenants pointed towards this future coming of the Messiah, God's Anointed One. Through all these Covenants we see a God who is willing to interact with his creation and bless it. When first century Christians such as Paul, Peter and John checked all the events surrounding the life of Jesus, they searched their Scriptures, our Old Testament. It was as the Holy Spirit illuminated their minds, that they wrote down and passed on the Old Testament promises which were fulfilled in God's Messiah and the world's hope: Jesus Christ and him alone. Jesus Christ fits all five of those principles referred to in the Old Testament Messiah. For example: 2 Samuel 7:12 predicts the birth of Solomon as David's successor to the throne with his role being to establish David's throne forever (2 Samuel 7:13). We see this link to Jesus Christ, though the genealogies to both Joseph: with a legal right to David's throne (Matthew 1:1-17) and to Mary: with a blood right to David's throne (Luke 3:23-38).

The Mosaic Covenant, which included the Law of Moses, was given to make them realize the helplessness of their own efforts, and their need of God's help for salvation. Galatians 3:22-24 explains that the Law was only a protective fence, until through the promised Messiah, humanity could be made right with God through faith. All of history pointed to the coming of this Messiah, this Christ. This was part of Paul's reasoning from Scripture with the Jews, that he met and conversed with. Of course, for Paul, as for us, the Messiah is Jesus Christ. Is there a conflict between God's law and God's promises? Absolutely not. If the Law could give us new life, we could be made right with God by obeying it. But the Scriptures declare that we are all prisoners of sin, so we receive God's promise of freedom only by believing in Jesus Christ.

Before the way of faith in Christ was available to humanity, the people of God were protected by the wall of the Law. It was meant to be a good thing defining the people of God and helping them to walk in his way. But, over the centuries it became a bad thing, serving only to keep non-Jewish people out of reach of fellowship with God. Other people, Gentiles, even if they wanted to, could only get into the people of God with great difficulty. Now that the way of faith has come, fellowship with God is freely available for all those who desire it, walking through the gateway opened by Jesus Christ on the Cross, having been declared right before God, wrapped in the robes of Jesus' own Sonship and righteousness.

> [26] For you are all children of God through faith in Christ Jesus. [27] And all who have been united with Christ in baptism have put on Christ, like putting on new clothes.
> (Galatians 3:26-27)

When Jesus cleansed the temple in John 2, Jesus was announcing that he was the Messiah. His disciples knew this to be a sign of Jesus being the

Christ Messiah. Psalm 69:9 predicted someone with a zeal to protect the honour of God's Temple. By behaving like this, Jesus was concerned for God's honour alone. Why? Because the Temple was considered to be where the Lord was in a very special way and therefore to the very centre of their religion. It was for prayer and worship – not for trading and profiteering.

The religious leaders also knew it as a sign, which is why they asked for a sign and a miracle to prove that Jesus had the authority to justify his actions. If Jesus did not give them a sign, he would merely be a lawbreaking troublemaker and rabble-rouser. Consequently, Jesus does offer them a sign - "tear down this temple, and I'll rebuild it in three days." (John 2:19). Of course, the religious leaders completely misunderstood what Jesus meant. The temple was still not complete, so how could he tear it down?

What Jesus actually meant is revealed by John, after the event. The temple Jesus was talking about was his own body. Throughout his public ministry, Jesus always had his crucifixion and resurrection as his goal. The sign that Jesus would give to the religious authorities was his own resurrection, three days after his death. The resurrection would be the final proof of Jesus being the Messiah they were waiting for.

Jesus' humanity

That Jesus was a human cannot really be disputed. Scripture says that he was born of a woman which in itself tells us that prenatally he was nurtured and formed in the womb as any other male baby was and is. His genealogical line is given. He grew into manhood as any young Jewish boy did. With his humanity, he exhibited normal human emotions such as love, weeping, sadness, anger and anguish. Jesus ate and drank. He had a body and a soul. He undertook the baptism of John, just as others had done. Jesus grew tired, he slept & perspired. Religiously, he worshipped as a Jew. Jesus died, just as all mortal people do. He was human in every way that we are - physically, mentally and emotionally. The only exception is that he was sinless. His humanity is beyond question, though unlike us, he was sinless.

Yet, could Jesus have sinned? If he was human, as we are suggesting, yet did not have the inherent sinful nature which all humans have from birth, then he could not be fully human. Yes, Jesus was tempted just as we are, but could Jesus really have succumbed to the tempter? While Jesus could have sinned, it was certain he would not. Jesus needed to be fully human for various reasons. These reasons include:

- His death would sacrificially atone for us
- He can empathize and pray for us
- Jesus exhibited true and perfect humanity
- due to his perfect humanity, Jesus is to be our example to follow
- true human nature is good
- Jesus shows that while God is transcendent, he is not so far removed from us that he can't interact with his creation

Jesus' deity

Jesus' deity and the Incarnation are central and basic teaching of historic Christianity as it is central to God's eternal plan of salvation. God's salvation plan for humans involved triumphant victory over sin, death and the grave. However no person could be found that was eligible or capable to do this. Because of this, God stepped into human history, so that this victory could be achieved.

This God-man would be fully human, so as to live every facet of humanity, including suffering and death. This God-man would also need to remain fully God, so as to defeat sin, death and the grave. Jesus, being sinless (Hebrews 4:15), was this unique God-man, consisting as he does of two complete natures: the God nature and the human nature.

Anselm, one of the Church fathers, observed that God had formed Adam without mother and father and had formed Eve without mother and father but from a man. So God could certainly form Jesus, without the usual sexual reproduction process, from a woman. Ergo, God stepped into human history. But what is the scriptural evidence for the claims regarding Jesus' deity.

The apostle John expressly calls Jesus, the Word (logos) or God. This logos became human and was the only begotten God. Later on in life John expressly states Jesus as "the true God and eternal life". John claims Jesus as having some of the attributes of God - eternal, life and truth.

Jesus himself claimed equality with God. When Jesus stated, "your sins are forgiven", the scribes attributed this as a God alone thing and thereby accused in their minds, Jesus of blasphemy. During his trial, when being questioned on a charge of blasphemy, Jesus equates himself with God. Other New Testament writers enhance this concept of Jesus being equal with God.

Thomas, when seeing Jesus post-resurrection, calls Jesus "My Lord and my God" (John 20:28). Paul exclaims Jesus as our "great God and Saviour" (Titus 2:13). The writer of Hebrews pronounces of Jesus that "Your throne, O God, endures forever and ever...." (Hebrews 1:8). Works of God are ascribed to him, as Creations' sustainer. Therefore we can be confidently assured that Jesus, whilst being fully man was also fully God.

Why would God become a man?

God himself has taken on the responsibility for our sins. Jesus on the Cross bore our sins, though he was sinless, and became sin for us. By doing this, we are drawn to him in a personal way. God has shown that he loves us and wants us in a relationship with himself. God has bridged the gap between the supernatural and the natural, the infinite and the finite, to show us what he is like. Jesus as God in person, gives us a focal point to respond to. God does not compel us to love him, but invites all to a dynamic relationship with Him.

God is one and therefore there could only be one incarnation. By doing away with the incarnation, how then could God's salvation plan be fulfilled? Not at all. If Jesus was not God, then he would be part of the problem and therefore need to be redeemed himself! Certainly an untenable proposition.

Two natures

Yet our inquisitive human minds ask another

question. How can somebody have both natures - deity and humanity? This was another question asked in the early Church, where they concluded that Jesus whilst being fully God, didn't lose any of that divinity when he became human. Instead of losing anything, Jesus gained humanity. This divine and human nature unity is called 'hypostatic union'. Early Church synods affirmed Jesus' two natures as well as his personal unity.

Jesus and you

This is the Jesus, David writes about in Psalm 2! This is the Jesus, Paul is writing about in his letter to the Church in Colossae. Colossians 3:1-4 describes perfectly our relationship with Jesus now, if we are Christians. What are we to do with this Jesus if we claim to be his followers and in relationship with him?

Christians, followers of Jesus, have died with Jesus Christ (Colossians 3:3). Paul expounds this fully in his letter to the Romans. Jesus not only died for us, but we died with him. Christ not only died for sin, but died unto sin to break its power. Through the work of the Holy Spirit we are in Christ. Through baptism, we symbolise death with Christ. We can conquer our old sinful nature if we want to.

Christians are raised with Christ (Colossians 3:1). Just as we symbolically died with Christ, we are symbolically raised with Christ in baptism. It is a fact that we are raised with him and we rule with him, seated at the right hand of the Father.

Christians live with Christ (Colossians 3:4). If we are Christian people, Jesus is our life and our eternal life, is Jesus. We are dead to sin, yet alive to Christ. Followers of Jesus are hidden spiritually with Christ (Colossians 3:3). For those of you who like a good mystery, here is one for you. We are hidden with Him! We no longer belong to this world, but we belong to Jesus Christ. We are hidden with him in heaven. That is not to say we are to neglect our earthly duties and responsibilities, but that our motives and strengths come from heaven.

Lastly, the Church, all followers of Jesus Christ, past, present and future, will be glorified with Jesus Christ (Colossians 3:4). When Jesus Christ comes again, and he is coming again, we will see him face to face. When Jesus comes again, he will take us home and we shall enter eternal glory with him. When Jesus Christ is revealed in glory, we too shall be revealed in glory. We already have some of this glory, but one day the full extent of this glorification will be revealed. What a day that will be!

Appendix 2: Assured Atonement

1 The Lord spoke to Moses after the death of Aaron's two sons, who died after they entered the Lord's presence and burned the wrong kind of fire before Him. 2 The Lord said to Moses, "Warn your brother, Aaron, not to enter the Most Holy Place behind the inner curtain whenever he chooses; if he does, he will die. For the Ark's cover—the place of atonement—is there, and I myself am present in the cloud above the atonement cover.

3 "When Aaron enters the sanctuary area, he must follow these instructions fully. He must bring a young bull for a sin offering and a ram for a burnt offering. 4 He must put on his linen tunic and the linen undergarments worn next to his body. He must tie the linen sash around his waist and put the linen turban on his head. These are sacred garments, so he must bathe himself in water before he puts them on. 5 Aaron must take from the community of Israel two male goats for a sin offering and a ram for a burnt offering.

6 "Aaron will present his own bull as a sin offering to purify himself and his family, making them right with the Lord. 7 Then he

must take the two male goats and present them to the Lord at the entrance of the Tabernacle. 8 He is to cast sacred lots to determine which goat will be reserved as an offering to the Lord and which will carry the sins of the people to the wilderness of Azazel. 9 Aaron will then present as a sin offering the goat chosen by lot for the Lord. 10 The other goat, the scapegoat chosen by lot to be sent away, will be kept alive, standing before the Lord. When it is sent away to Azazel in the wilderness, the people will be purified and made right with the Lord. (Leviticus 16:1-10)

Leviticus 16 describes the Day of Atonement which was to occur annually on the tenth day of the seventh month. We know that God had chosen Israel to be his people and that they were supposed to be a shining beacon of light and hope to the world. As part of the covenant made with Moses, God said that he would be their God and they would be his people. What a contrast to the nations around them that worshipped multiple 'gods', made of material such as wood or stone and often thirsty for human sacrifice. Contrast those 'gods', with the God of Israel, who had made himself personally present with his people in the Tent of Meeting or Tabernacle. Let's look briefly at what went on at this Day of Atonement or Yom Kippur.

The Tabernacle / Tent of Meetings: Most of the activity takes place in the Tabernacle. What did the Tabernacle look like? The Tabernacle, or as it is also known the Tent of Meeting, was a part canvas, part wooden marquee divided across the middle by a curtain. There was the 'public' side and the other side, beyond the curtain, known as the Holy of Holies, where only the Chief Priest could enter and that only once a year. Inside the Holy of Holies, included the

- Mercy Seat (Atonement Cover): the removable top of the Ark where the blood was sprinkled by the High Priest

- Ark of the Covenant: a small chest or box representing God's presence with his people
- Golden Censer: Aaron, the High Priest used this to make the cloud of smoky incense as he entered the Holy of Holies. This was to form a wall of protection for Aaron, hiding God from Aaron. To look directly upon God would have caused Aaron's death. The smoke and incense ensured that God's holiness was bearable to sinful man, that God's mystery remained, and Aaron was preserved.

So what is this Day of Atonement all about? Leviticus 16:1-10 gives us a summary. To atone means to clean, make amends, and to substitute. Leviticus 16 starts by referring back to an incident with Abihu and Nadab who died as a result of their sin of offering unauthorised worship to God (Leviticus 10).

Through their death, the Lord God states the fundamental principles for priests – only priests could therefore mediate for the nation before him and they had to be spiritually and ceremonially clean. In that way, the priests would not commit the same sin as Abihu and Nadab had done nor suffer the same consequence.

The Offerings

There were 5 offerings performed on the Day of Atonement in order to cleanse and re-consecrate the Tabernacle. All included the death of an animal and therefore involved blood. There were

- 2 blood-atonement sin offerings for priests and people (Leviticus 16 3, 5, 11-19)
- 1 scapegoat sin offering for everybody (Leviticus 16 5, 7-10, 20-22)
- 2 burnt offerings for priests and people (Leviticus 16 23-24)

Blood

"[11] for the life of the body is in its blood. I have given you the blood on the altar to purify you, making you right with the LORD. It is the blood, given in exchange for a life, that makes purification possible."
(Leviticus 17:11)

How is the life in the blood? Today, most of us here are probably a bit squeamish when it comes to blood. But here is what blood consists of and the job that it does. The liquid part is called plasma, which consists of water, salts, and protein. Over half of blood is plasma. The solid part of blood contains red blood cells, white blood cells, and platelets. Red blood cells deliver oxygen to organs, cells and tissues. They also provide essential nutrients such as amino acids, fatty acids, and glucose all the while removing waste materials, such as carbon dioxide, urea, and lactic acid. The white blood cells meanwhile protect the body from infection and foreign bodies. As for the platelets, they are there to plug a wound while the clotting cascade gets to work to form a more permanent clot. Any platelet missing and the clotting fails. And do you know why blood is red? Because of the iron! That is why there is life in the blood.

But why was blood used to 'cleanse' or atone? Why not water? Did God need blood, as some form of bloodlust or to quench his thirst for blood? No! Not at all. God didn't need blood, but blood was used to show that sin had a cost – the cost was blood because life is in the blood (Leviticus 17:11). The substitution of a dead animal reflected a temporary covering or veneer, which is why it needed to be done over and over again.

All these sacrifices, cleansings and ceremonies were to be done, not for the sake of God but as pictures for his people to make them understand how serious sin was and how difficult it was to provide a remedy for it. The nation of Israel was to be a shining light for God to the other nations. Israel were to show that God is One, a living and personal God, and not an impersonal 'god' made of stone or wood of human construction.

Aaron

During his normal daily duties, he represented God before the people, and was dressed as a king. To signal that, he would wear grand clothes which signified the high honour in which he was held. Therefore, Aaron was ordinarily dressed in very special clothes to signify that high honour and duty as God's representative to the people of Israel.

However, on this one day of the year, the Day of Atonement, Aaron represented the people before God. Before the Lord Almighty, Aaron is stripped of honour and is dressed as a servant. Verse 4 shows us he is to be wearing a simple linen tunic covering simple linen undergarments, with a linen sash around himself and a linen turban on his head.

Why? In order to approach God as a servant. So, to a certain extent, Aaron was a servant King. Look at v3. A direct command: "This is how Aaron is to enter the Most Holy Place." You can be sure that Aaron would enter carefully, respectfully and reverently. Before he could go into the most holy place, he had to create an obscuring cloud of incense in the Holy of Holies, to veil the glory of

God so he could enter and live. No doubt the memory of his sons, Abihu and Nadab provided an extra incentive to follow God's rules meticulously.

Scapegoat

Then there is the remarkable story of the scapegoat. There were 2 goats to be offered. One goat was sacrificed as a substitutionary sin offering for the people and its blood taken into the Holy of Holies and sprinkled on the mercy seat. Aaron laid his hands on the second goat's head, the one kept alive, and symbolically cast the burden of sins of the nation onto the goat. It was then driven out into the wilderness, far away from the camp and was never to return. In this remarkable dual picture the people were shown that their sins were atoned for and also removed far out of sight into the wilderness.

The people: Lastly, what about the people? What were they to do? Just sit there and be bored while all this took place? No. They were not to be passive but rather to actively observe a special and very complete Sabbath rest. They were to remember this day as a permanent addition to their annual calendar by "denying themselves" for the day or "humbling their souls" as another translation puts v31. This involved not doing routine things such as working and feasting. They were also to trust that Aaron was being fully obedient to the regulations as given by God. They were to ponder upon the awesomeness of their God that lived amongst them, and to reflect upon the cost of their sin and disobedience.

Atonement Complete

On this Day of Atonement, the one day of the year, Atonement took place between God and his people. No wonder there were great scenes of celebration after! God would continue to live with his people! A cause for celebration! WOW! Atonement means both a sacrifice and a cleansing. God's holy dwelling place and all things associated with it were cleansed.

The sins and disobedience of the nation of Israel, over the previous year, had left impurities as stipulated in Leviticus 16:16. The cleansing blood was to symbolise the great cost of sin. But now on this one day, all has been cleansed, forgiven and forgotten! All sins, both for the nation of Israel as a whole and for all individuals, were wiped clean and forgiven! Alleluia! If that is atonement, a reasonable question to ask, is why is there a need for atonement? What does all that mean for us today?

Atonement Today (Hebrews 9-10)

We see in the creation story from Genesis, that Almighty God created the Universe and all that is in it, including our Planet Earth. Upon this Earth, God has created countless species of animals, fish , birds and everything in between. There are 400,000 different species of plants. All formed with an utterance by God.

Even more wondrous though, is that God created humanity in his own likeness and image. You and me. No two humans, in all of history, are completely the same, despite outward appearances. Every day, each of us produces 200 billion new red blood cells and our blood travels 12,000 miles within our body.

The total length of all the nerves in your body is 47 miles. There is enough DNA in your body alone, that if decompressed, it would wrap around the diameter of our Solar System twice. We are fearfully and wonderfully made. Did you feel that last incoming brain impulse you just had? It was travelling at a speed of about 250 mph. Incredible! That is you and me! WOW!

There we are. In the beginning, God and humanity were in relationship. There was an innate intimacy between God and humanity. However, shortly after their creation, humanity disobeyed

God's clear command. Humanity said: "You know what, God. I love you but I think my way is best, so I am going to go do that." Humanity went ahead with their own way, and in an act of disobedience, sinned against Almighty God. You can read about that in Genesis 3. The relationship was broken and afterwards there was nothing humanity could do about it, in order to restore that relationship between God and humanity.

As we have seen together, that is the story of this broken world. A world which is in a mess. Even a cursory look around will tell you that. God could have just said "Oh well. I will just leave them to it." But he didn't do that! Because he is a God of love, God himself needed to intervene, so that humanity could choose to return to being in an active, dynamic and intimate relationship with God. The Old Testament traces that journey, and that is where we are with the story before us with Moses, Aaron and the people of ancient Israel.

One principle of reading the Bible, as I am sure you are aware, is to let the Bible interpret the Bible. Bearing that in mind, Hebrews 9 & 10 are the best commentary on Leviticus 16. In there we see that Jesus Christ is our scapegoat and has taken the immense burden of our sins on himself. It is no coincidence therefore that Jesus died outside the city as the writer points out in Hebrews 13:12.

Aaron was a type of servant king as we saw, but Jesus was the ultimate servant king. Aaron, as Chief Priest, offered sacrifices for the cleansing of sin, including his own disobediences. But Jesus Christ himself was both the sacrifice and the Chief Priest. Jesus Christ who was sinless and had led a perfect life of obedience to God, became sin. Why would Jesus Christ – fully God and fully human – become sin?

We saw that the Day of Atonement was held once a year. Atonement as achieved by Jesus Christ, was the unique, the one and only, unrepeatable, Day of Calvary which we celebrate at Easter. It is what we remember when taking the Holy Communion. That is why the bread and wine only symbolize Jesus' body and blood. If it were more than symbolic, then it would be like a repeat of his death each time. Certainly untenable. There is only one day of Calvary and on that historical day, Jesus' death was the once and for all atoning and substitutionary sacrifice, which makes amends to God for the sins of the world. Jesus alone, gives life and offers life to the full – a life borne from grace and not from Law. Jesus ushered in the New Covenant, which we looked at last week.

At the time of Jesus, the Temple was the Tabernacle's successor in Jerusalem. In the Temple, there was a curtain as thick as a hand in the Holy of

Holies to prevent anyone entering the Holy Place unauthorized. Perhaps with the lesson of Nadab and Abihu in mind. When Jesus died on the Cross, that curtain to the Holy of Holies in the Temple, was torn in two from top to bottom. This was to symbolize that access to God was now open to all who enter by faith. All because of Jesus of Nazareth.

As we have hopefully seen, in the Old Testament, under the Law, sins were dealt with by blood sacrifices of atonement as coverings for sin, for without the shedding of blood there can be no forgiveness. Sin is a word that has come down in the world. Sin is seen by some people as something to do with particularly sleazy parts of a city or town, or something only convicted felons actually do. However, as we have already seen, sin is in fact any disobedience against God – in thought, word, action, inaction or attitude. A blood sacrifice was God's way of dealing with sin, to show the true cost of sin.

However, the solution as we have also hopefully seen, lies not in the continual animal sacrifices of the Old Testament because Hebrews 10:4 reminds us that the blood of animals cannot take away sin but was only ever a veneer or covering. That was why it was necessary to repeat them time and time again. It is only through the death of Jesus, that sin is taken away (Hebrews 9:11-15, 24-28), and that was only needed once. The annual Day of Atonement was looking forward to the coming of a Messiah, who as we know, is the man we know as Jesus Christ.

Therefore, Jesus is the permanent sacrificial substitute. Jesus, the Lamb of God, was the atonement for all sin – past, present and future. Therefore, it is his atonement which results in salvation for all people who are prepared to accept his work on their behalf. Nothing we can do can earn us salvation from God's judgement of our sin. It is a free gift from God, from his wellsprings of grace and mercy. But we have to accept it and take it as a gift.

Jesus as God in person, gives humanity a focal point to respond to. God does not force people to love him, but he invites all people to be in a dynamic relationship with him. God is love, but God will not force people against their will to be in a relationship with himself, but his love is compelling. Love never forces but it always calls, seeks and is compelling. There is a difference. Each person can choose for themselves if they want to take up this offer, or not. The free offer of forgiveness is available to all who choose to accept it... Amazing love shown by an Almighty God of love. Let's now look a little further into Jesus' atonement for sin. We have looked to a degree already, but it is worth to be reminded again.

Propitiation: Jesus was the propitiation for all sin! This is a difficult word for our modern minds. Propitiation means the turning aside of God's anger by the offering of the sacrifice of Christ. Now we must remember that with sin and the consequences of sin, God is angry (Psalm 7:11) and rightly so. Towards sin and sinful behaviour, we know that God has great fury, anger and wrath (Jeremiah 21:5). We are reminded by the writer to the Hebrews, that it is a terrible thing to fall into the hands of the living God (Hebrews 10:3-31). Yet as Micah elucidates to us in relation to this:

Where is another God like you,
who pardons the guilt of the remnant,
overlooking the sins of his special people?
You will not stay angry with your people forever, because you delight in showing unfailing love.
(Micah 7:18)

God's anger and judgment of all sin falls on Jesus Christ, instead of on humanity. To accept this, we need to approach God so that his anger is appeased (Isaiah 53:5; Romans 3:25; Hebrews 2:17; 1 John 2:2). It is a free gift, but a gift, needs to be opened in order for it to be truly received.

Redemption

Not only was it a propitiation, but it was also an act of redemption!   In the time of the New Testament, this word was used to refer to the buying back of a slave - the price paid to buy the slave's freedom. God paid the redemption price so that humans can be freed from their slavery to sin (John 8:35, 36, Romans 6:17-19; 7:14). The price was paid (1 Peter 1:18-19) and so we are redeemed and bought with the precious blood of Jesus the Christ (1 Corinthians 6:19-20). Again, that should cause you to go WOW and thank God.

Substitution

Jesus died for our sin, the just for the unjust, or the righteous for the unrighteous says the Apostle Peter in 1 Peter 3:18. That is how God is both just and the Justifier of sinners. That is why Jesus needed to be both fully God and fully human! If he lacked either, it would not be the full substitutionary sacrifice that was necessary to bear the permanent consequences of sin! If he was not God, his death would only be of value for himself. If he was not human, then he would not be a sufficient and satisfactory substitute for us. The Scriptures tell us, that for while we were yet sinners, Jesus Christ died for us, (Romans 5:6-8), willingly giving his life as a ransom for us (Mark 10:45) and when he died in our place on the Cross at Calvary, he bore the consequences and judgement of all sin – past, present and future. This substitution was the sacrifice, 'at-one-ment' or sin offering, required in order that Jesus as the Lamb of God could take away the sins of the world (John 1:29). He, Jesus, therefore, became sin (2 Corinthians 5:21) because it was his blood as a Lamb without spot or blemish (1 Peter 1:18-19), shed on the Cross at his death, that fulfils God's requirements permanently. Amazingly WOW isn't it? Sometimes though, we are reminded of the sins for which we have asked forgiveness. The perpetrators of this could be satan, other people or our own conscience. We do have to bear the consequences of our sins but not the eternal judgement of them before Almighty God. Yet the Bible tells us

> [21] And since we have a great High Priest who rules over God's house, [22] let us go right into the presence of God with sincere hearts fully trusting him. For our guilty consciences have been sprinkled with Christ's blood to make us clean, and our bodies have been washed with pure water.
> (Hebrews 10:21-22)

We declare to our detractors that our confessed sins are forgiven. Those sins may have consequences but of themselves, those sins are in the wilderness as far as the East is from the West. Amazing love. We are forgiven! Forgiveness is freedom! Freedom from fear and freedom from judgement. True forgiveness is not just saying sorry. Forgiveness includes penitence and also a desire never to do that same thing again.

Propitiation, redemption and sacrifice can be summed up in one word - Love. God loves humanity. As Christians, we are bought at a price, and we have a new position before God! We are bought out of slavery to sin, into glorious freedom where we are now slaves to Jesus Christ and righteousness (Romans 6:19, 22). We are also Jesus Christ's personal possession (1 Corinthians 6:19). But it is our responsibility to choose that way! God does not coerce forcefully – he leaves it as a choice for us humans to make as individuals. What is our response to this to be? Love – Love God and love others actively. More about that next week.

Because of Jesus, and only because of Jesus, God accepts us as his children and comes to live within us. Isn't that amazing? I still find it amazing even after being a Christian now for over 35 years. God comes to live within us, and it is all because of the atoning work of God the Son, Jesus Christ, in his death on the Cross. Amazing. Do you know this God? Isn't that a cause for a WOW of joy? Atoning joy! Joy, the amazing quiet and inner confidence that we can have, knowing we are his children and he is our God. WOW!

My Jesus

Jesus Christ - unique, majestic, tender, wise, strong, and lovely. This Jesus who is always there to help me, wipe my tears, give me joy, relieve my frustrations, give clarity over confusion and give me peace. Is this also your Jesus? That is my Jesus, whom I seek to serve and obey in every facet of life of every day. I rarely achieve it for more than moments, but I know that when I fail, I can ask for forgiveness and he will grant it from his wellsprings of love, grace and mercy.

It is this Jesus whom I depend upon and personally know to be totally reliable in every way. When people let me down, turn away from me, discourage me, think wrongly off me, incorrectly assume my motives, this Jesus always picks me up, never turns me away, always encourages and embraces me. He comforts me. He challenges me., At the end of each day, I know that all through each day, that Jesus has been dependable, going ahead of me. Amazing that somebody could love me like that. Do you know Him? If we would call ourselves a Christian, a follower and disciple of the Jesus Christ, we know that we are being transformed into the image of Jesus and will continue to be until Jesus returns once more for us and for his body, the Church. Sometimes this transformation takes comfort and at other times we need to be challenged. Remember, our God challenges us in our comfort and comforts us in our challenges. Or is that just my experience? Do you know Him?

Appendix 3: Harmony Of Easter

With the Gospel accounts, we can get a broad scope of all the events of Jesus life here on earth, obviously including the events of Easter, as listed below. Look at all the people involved, the actions and events, all of which help make Easter amazing.

- Jesus' farewell teaching: John 15:1-16:33
- Jesus prays for his disciples: John 17:1-26
- Jesus enters Gethsemane: Matthew 26:36; Mark 14:32; Luke 22:39-40; John 18:1
- Jesus prays in the Garden of Gethsemane: Matthew 26:36-46; Mark 14:32-42; Luke 22:40-46
- Crowd of people come to arrest Jesus: Matthew 26:47; Mark 14;43; John 18:2-3
- Judas betrays Jesus with a kiss: Matthew 26:48-50; Mark 14:44-45; Luke 22:47-48
- Jesus answers the mob with authority: John 18:4-9
- Peter severs the ear of Malchus: Matthew 26:50-54; Mark 14:46-47; Luke 22:49-50; John 18:10-11
- Jesus heals Malchus; Luke 22:51
- Jesus is arrested and the disciples flee: Matthew 26:55-56; Mark 14:48-52; Luke 22:52-54; John 18:12
- Jesus is led to the High Priest's house: Matthew 26:57; Mark 14:53; Luke 22:54; John 18:13-14
- Peter follows at a distance: Matthew 26:58; 14:54; Luke 22:54; John 18:15-16
- Peter's 1st denial – door-keeping girl: Matthew 26:69-70; Mark 14:66-68; Luke 22:55-57; John 18:17-18

- Annas questions Jesus: John 18:19-24
- Peter's 2nd denial - by the fire: Matthew 26:71-72; Mark 14:69-70; Luke 22:58; John 18:25
- Peter's 3rd denial - relative of Malchus: Matthew 26:73-75; Mark 14:70-72; Luke 22:59-62; John 18:26-27
- Guards beat Jesus: Luke 22:63-65
- False witnesses testify: Matthew 26:59-61; Mark 14:55-59
- Caiaphas condemns Jesus: Matthew 26:62-66; Mark 14:60-64; Luke 22:66-71
- Sanhedrin beats Jesus: Matthew 26:67-68; Mark 14:65
- Jesus lead from Caiaphas to Praetorium: John 18:28
- Remorse of Judas: Matthew 27:1-10; Acts 1:16-20
- Jesus before Pilate: Matthew 27:1-14; Luke 23:1-7; John 18:29-38
- Jesus before Herod; Luke 23:8-10
- Herod's soldiers mock Jesus: Mark 15:1-5; Luke 23:11-12
- Pilate releases Barabbas: Matthew 27:15-26; Mark 15:6-15; Luke 23:13-25; John 18:38-40
- Pilate's soldiers crown Jesus and mock him: Matthew 27:27-30; Mark 15:16-20; John 19:1-3

- Pilate tries to release Jesus: John 19:4-7
- Pilate questions Jesus again: John 19:8-11
- Pilate tries to release Jesus again: John 19:12
- Pilate sentences Jesus: John 19:13-15
- Pilate delivers Jesus to be crucified: John 19:16
- Jesus carries his cross: John 19:17
- Simon of Cyrene bears Jesus' cross: Matthew 27:31-32; Mark 15:20-21; Luke 23:26
- Jesus speaks to the weeping women; Luke 23:27-32
- Jesus is brought to Golgotha: Matthew 27:33; Mark 15:22; Luke 23:32-33; John 19:17
- Soldiers offer Jesus a sour wine mix: Matthew 27:34; Mark 15:23
- Jesus is crucified on the 3rd hour: Mark 15:25
- 2 robbers are crucified with Jesus: Matthew 27:38; Mark 15:27-28; Luke 23:33; John 19:18
- Inscription written by Pilate: Matthew 27:37; Mark 15:26; Luke 23:38; John 19:19-22
- Jesus says, "Forgive them...": Luke 23:34
- Soldiers divide the garments of Jesus: Matthew 27:35-36; Mark 15:24; Luke 23:34; John 19:23-24
- Jesus says, "Behold your mother.": John 19:25-27
- Multitudes mock Jesus: Matthew 27:39-43; Mark 15:29-32; Luke 23:35-37

- Robbers mock Jesus: Matthew 27:44; Mark 15:32; Luke 23:39
- One robber rebukes the other; Luke 23:40-41
- Jesus says to one robber "...you will be with me in Paradise."; Luke 23:43
- Darkness from 6th to 9th hour: Matthew 27:45; Mark 15:33; Luke 23:44-45
- Jesus cries out "My God! My God! Why have you abandoned me?": Matthew 27:46; Mark 15:34
- Jesus says, "I thirst.": John 19:28
- Jesus is offered sour wine on a reed: Matthew 27:47-49; Mark 15:35-36; John 19:29-30
- Jesus cries out "It is finished.": John 19:30
- Jesus cries out "Into Your hands I commit my spirit.": Matthew 27:50; Mark 15:37; Luke 23:46
- Jesus bows his head and dies: Matthew 27:50; Mark 15:37; Luke 23:46; John 19:30
- Temple veil torn from top to bottom: Matthew 27:51; Mark 15:38; Luke 23:45
- Earthquake: Matthew 27:51
- Saints rise, after Christ's resurrection: Matthew 27:52-53
- Centurion glorifies God: Matthew 27:54; Mark 15:39; Luke 23:47
- Multitude which witnessed Jesus' death,

leave grieving: Luke 23:48

- Women watch from a distance: Matthew 27:55-56; Mark 15:40-41: Luke 23:49
- Request that Jesus' legs be broken: John 19:31-32
- Soldier pierces Jesus' side: John 19:33-34
- Fulfilment of prophecy: John 19:35-37
- Joseph requests body from Pilate: Matthew 27:57-58; Mark 15:42-43; Luke 23:50-52; John 19:38
- Centurion reports that Jesus is dead: Mark 15:44-45
- Joseph takes Jesus' body: Mark 15:45; John 19:38
- Nicodemus and Joseph prepare Jesus' body: John 19:39-40
- Jesus' body placed in new garden tomb: Matthew 27:59-60; Mark 15:46; Luke 23:53; John 19:41-42
- Two Mary's watch the burial of Jesus: Matthew 27:61; Mark 15:47; Luke 23:54-55
- Roman soldiers guard Jesus' tomb: Matthew 27:62-66
- The two Mary's prepare spices for Jesus' body and then rest: Luke 23:56
- Angel rolls stone away from Jesus' tomb: Matthew 28:2-4
- Women bring spices to Jesus' tomb at dawn:

Matthew 28:1; Mark 16:1-4; Luke 24:1-3; John 20:1

- Angels appear to women: Matthew 28:5-7; Mark 16:5-7; Luke 24:4-8
- Women run to tell the disciples: Matthew 28:8; Mark 16:8; Luke 24:9-11; John 20:2
- Peter and John run to the tomb and inspect the empty interior: Luke 24:12; John 20:3-9
- Peter and John go home: Luke 24:12; John 20:10
- Mary Magdalene stands weeping: John 20:11
- Mary sees two angels: John 20:12-13
- Jesus appears to Mary Magdalene: Mark 16:9; John 20:14-17
- Jesus appears to other women: Matthew 28:9-10
- Women report to the disciples: Mark 16:10-11; John 20:18
- Guards report to the priests: Matthew 28:11-15
- Jesus meets two people on the Emmaus road: Mark 16:12-13; Luke 24:13-32
- Jesus appears to Peter: Luke 24:34
- Two men Jesus talked to on the Emmaus road, report to the disciples in Jerusalem: Luke 24:33-35
- Jesus appears to the disciples without

Thomas: Luke 24:36-46; John 20:19-24
- Disciples report to Thomas: John 20:25
- Jesus appears to the disciples and Thomas: Mark 16:14; John 20:26-29
- Jesus appears to seven disciples by the sea: John 21:1-14
- Jesus questions Peter 3 times: John 21:15-23
- Jesus appears to a crowd of at least 500 people; 1 Corinthians 15:6
- Jesus appears to James: 1 Corinthians 15:7
- Jesus commissions the disciples: Matthew 28:16-20; Mark 16:15-18; Luke 24:44-49
- Jesus is received into Heaven: Mark 16:19-20; Luke 24:50-53
- John's first testimony: John 20:30-31
- John's second testimony: John 21:24-25

Becoming A Christian

If you want to turn to God right now, there is no need for delay. God is ready and willing to take you as his own right now. You only have to ask him to forgive you and to give you help on the journey ahead which he will do by giving you the gift of the Holy Spirit. It is a nurturing and personal partnership between God and yourself.

The act of deciding to change course in mid-life, is what is called conversion. You may also know it as being born again or deciding to be a Christian. When you place your faith in Jesus, becoming utterly dependent upon him, you turn to God. That means that you have changed your intentions in the way you are going to live in future.

However, once you have made that decision, you leave behind your spiritual isolation and rebellion against him. As you live each day, becoming more involved with Jesus day by day, you will discover you are changing. You will find yourself doing things that please Jesus and developing your relationship with him.

Until you enter a personal relationship with God, accepting his gift of salvation for yourself, sin (all that which alienates you from God), controls your rebellion against him. This sin is seen in your attitudes and your activities. God asks you to accept his management and guidance of your life. When you do that, God's point of view and his strength become your point of view and your source of strength. You turn your mind, will and heart to him for all you do.

If you want to become a Christian and start a new life of adventure following Jesus Christ, you need to open the gift of grace for yourself in order to receive it.

There are three simple steps to take:

- **Admit** that you have done wrong against God and his ways and turn away from those attitudes.

- **Believe** and trust in Jesus as your Saviour from the consequences of the anger of God towards you and your tendency to sin. Call on him, receive, trust, obey and worship him, recognizing him for who he is and what he has done.

- **Accept** the Holy Spirit of God into your life as the major motivating force for what you do. Once sin has been confessed, Jesus is believed in and trusted as Saviour then God the Holy Spirit has entered your life, then you are a Christian.

All these things happen together instantly as you turn to God, being ready to grow in the grace and knowledge of Jesus! That is a WOW moment in your life. Welcome to the family of God. God has chosen you; Jesus has paid for you and has put his mark within you through the Holy Spirit (Ephesians 1:1-13).

Once you have made that decision, you leave behind your rebellion against him. As you live each day, becoming more involved with Jesus day by day, you will find yourself changing. You stop doing things which separated you from him and find yourself doing things that develop your relationship with him. How do you develop this relationship?

Until you enter that relationship, sin, or that which alienates you from God, controls your rebellion against him in your attitudes and your activities. You develop this relationship by allowing God to take control of your life, as he asks you to accept his management and guidance of your life. God's point of view and his strength will become your point of view and your source of strength. You turn your mind, will and heart to him for all you do.

About The Author

I was born in a small country town in Australia. I was raised to be a sceptical agnostic/atheist with the words "Churches are dangerous places" ringing in my ears. Coming into my teenage years, I decided if Churches are so dangerous, let's rebel and go for a bit of danger. I rebelled, became a Christian, started attending a local Christian youth group and was baptized...

In 1990, I came to the UK for 6 months' travel around Europe. Or so I thought. I have stayed ever since. I view it as God having a sense of humour. He knows I don't like rain, cold and in particular - together. He has even given me the most beautiful of women as a wife, but she doesn't like hot weather. God sure has a sense of humour.

In 2003, I had a stroke and I took redundancy from my job. I went off to Moorlands College where I graduated in 2007. Later that year, I set up Partakers. At the end of 2018, we have had over 4 million unique visitors to the site, and had over 1 million resources downloaded. I currently reside with my wife in Bournemouth in the UK. I travel often to speak in places including the USA and Australia and would love to come and see you. I hope you have enjoyed this book and perhaps learnt something afresh or as a reminder. Please do contact me if you need clarification or disagree with something that is written here.

Peace and blessings.

Dave.

Other Books About Jesus By This Author

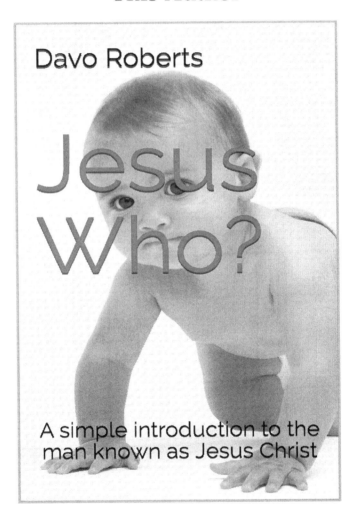

Davo Roberts

Jesus Who?

A simple introduction to the man known as Jesus Christ

A GLIMPSE
OF GOD
A look at Jesus Christ
the man who splits history

Dave G Roberts

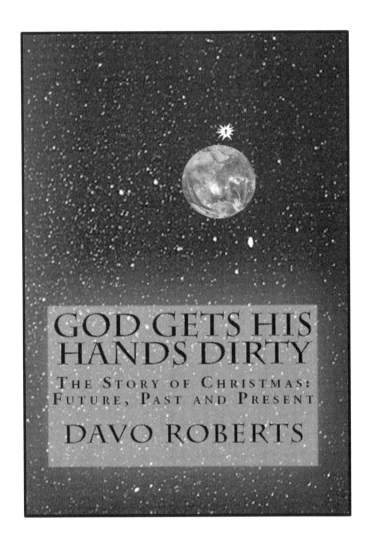

Read this
book to learn
more about
Jesus Christ

Davo Roberts

Other Books By This Author

AGOG: A Glimpse Of God: A Straight Look At The Man Who Splits History...

An Ambassador In God's Orchestra Of Joy

Dear Christian - Get A Good Grip: Basic Studies About God And Following Him

Dear Church: Wake Up: Issues Facing The Church Today

Developing Intimacy With God: A Little Book Of 95 Prayers

Exploring The Bible: A Simple Guide To The Story Of God And Humanity

God Gets his Hands Dirty

God, Internet Church & You

God's WOW Words For You: Straight Talk About Jesus And The Bible

Helping The Forgotten Church

Heroes And Heretics Abound: The Making Of The Modern Christian Church

Jesus Who? The Story of Christmas

Living Life Right: Studies In Romans 12

Scriptural Delights: Exploring Psalm 119

What's It All About Alphy? The Lord's Prayer: WOW Words Of The Bible

Glimpses Into Series

- Leviticus: A Book Of Joy
- 1 & 2 Chronicles: Books Of Heritage And History
- Psalms: A Book Of Life
- Song Of Songs: A Book Of Relationship
- Ezekiel: A Book Of Symbols And Visions.
- The Gospels: Books Of Good News
- Acts: A Book Of Action
- Romans: A Book Of Freedom

Read This Book Series:

- Volume 1: God Of The Bible
- Volume 2: Jesus Christ
- Volume 3: Being A Christian
- Volume 4: The Church
- Volume 5: Evangelism

All books are available in Paperback and Kindle at:

- PulpTheology.co.uk
- PulpTheology.com
- And all Amazon sites

About Partakers

Vision Statement: Partakers exists to communicate and disseminate resources for the purposes of Christian Discipleship, Evangelism and Worship by employing radical and relevant methods, including virtual reality and online distribution.

Mission Statement: To help the world, one person at a time, to engage in whole life discipleship, as Partakers of Jesus Christ.

Contact us to see how we can help you! Seminars, coaching, preaching, teaching, discipleship or evangelism – offline or online!

Website: http://www.partakers.co.uk
email: dave@partakers.co.uk
Mobile: 0794 794 5511

Printed in Great Britain
by Amazon